FINANCIAL INTEGRATION AND MACROFINANCIAL LINKAGES IN ASIA
CRISES, RESPONSES, AND POLICY CONSIDERATIONS

OCTOBER 2020

ASIAN DEVELOPMENT BANK

ADB

© 2020 Asian Development Bank
6 ADB Avenue, Mandaluyong City, 1550 Metro Manila, Philippines
Tel +63 2 8632 4444; Fax +63 2 8636 2444
www.adb.org

Some rights reserved. Published in 2020.

ISBN 978-92-9262-418-7 (print); 978-92-9262-419-4 (electronic); 978-92-9262-420-0 (ebook)
Publication Stock No. TCS200287-2
DOI: http://dx.doi.org/10.22617/TCS200287-2

The views expressed in this publication are those of the authors and do not necessarily reflect the views and policies of the Asian Development Bank (ADB) or its Board of Governors or the governments they represent.

ADB does not guarantee the accuracy of the data included in this publication and accepts no responsibility for any consequence of their use. The mention of specific companies or products of manufacturers does not imply that they are endorsed or recommended by ADB in preference to others of a similar nature that are not mentioned.

By making any designation of or reference to a particular territory or geographic area, or by using the term "country" in this document, ADB does not intend to make any judgments as to the legal or other status of any territory or area.

Corrigenda to ADB publications may be found at http://www.adb.org/publications/corrigenda.

Notes:
In this publication, "$" refers to United States dollars.
ADB recognizes "China" as the People's Republic of China.

Cover design by Erickson Mercado.

Contents

Tables, Figures, and Boxes

Foreword

Increasing financial interconnectedness in Asia and beyond over the past 2 decades has generated economic benefits, but, at the same time, increased the region's financial vulnerability. Financial contagion across closely interconnected financial markets has been all too vivid during recent financial crises. It is, therefore, important that policy makers understand the extent of financial interconnectedness and its macrofinancial implications when they consider macroeconomic policies. Likewise, they need to coordinate policy responses to prevent a buildup of systemic risk and enhance financial stability and resilience.

In this spirit, this report investigates the trends and patterns of cross-border financial linkages and their regulatory and policy implications. It finds that greater financial interconnectedness coincides with crisis periods, suggesting a possible source of financial contagion. This interconnectedness then declines, however, after financial volatility has subsided. The study also finds that banking exposures to crisis-affected advanced economies can trigger capital outflows across emerging economies. In addition, a buildup in distressed assets risks financial contagion, with spillover effects on macroeconomic conditions.

Domestically, macroprudential policies such as countercyclical measures, capital and liquidity buffers, and balance sheet instruments can reduce the procyclicality of financial systems.

Regionally, measures such as the Chiang Mai Initiative Multilateralization and associated regional macroeconomic surveillance through the ASEAN+3 Macroeconomic Research Office are helping strengthen Asia's financial safety net. Deepening local currency bond markets, through the Asian Bond Markets Initiative, also contributes to the region's financial stability and resilience by lessening the region's reliance on overseas borrowing for its long-term development.

Asia has made impressive progress in banking and financial health since the Asian and global financial crises. The coronavirus disease (COVID-19) pandemic and resultant accumulation of financial risks, however, call attention to the unfinished reform agenda in the region. This includes establishing comprehensive macroprudential policy tools and frameworks, developing deep and liquid local currency bond markets, and strengthening regional financial safety nets.

Advances in financial technologies and digital platforms also pose new challenges. They can bridge financial inclusion gaps and enhance efficiency of financial transactions, but they also pose security and interconnected risks to financial stability. Policy makers need to carefully balance the innovations and risks with informed regulation.

All of these underscore the need for coordinated efforts to enhance financial resilience and safeguard financial stability in highly interconnected financial markets and systems.

We should never let a crisis go to waste. I hope this report can help galvanize reforms to deal with existing and emerging challenges.

Yasuyuki Sawada
Chief Economist and Director General
Economic Research and Regional Cooperation Department
Asian Development Bank

Acknowledgments

This report was prepared by the Asian Development Bank (ADB) Regional Cooperation and Integration Division (ERCI) of the Economic Research and Regional Cooperation Department under the supervision of Cyn-Young Park, director of ERCI, with support from TA 9210: Enhancing Research Alliance and South–South Development Policy Cooperation Between Asia and the Pacific and Latin America.

The main authors of the report include Junkyu Lee, Peter Rosenkranz, and Josef T. Yap. Paulo Rodelio Halili and Monica Melchor provided excellent economic research and technical support.

This report greatly benefited from the theme chapter of the 2017 Asian Economic Integration Report "The Era of Financial Interconnectedness: How Can Asia Strengthen Financial Resilience?", which guides the discussion. It also draws from background studies provided for the theme chapter, prepared by Ross Buckley, Stijn Claessens, Mardi Dungey, Junkyu Lee, Cyn-Young Park, Peter Rosenkranz, Kwanho Shin, and James Villafuerte.

Peter Rosenkranz and Paulo Rodelio Halili coordinated the production of this report.

Eric Van Zant edited the manuscript, Erickson Mercado created the cover design, and Edith Creus implemented the typesetting and layout. Monina Gamboa proofread the report, while Marjorie Celis handled the page proof checking. The Printing Services Unit of ADB's Office of Administrative Services and the Publishing Team of the Department of Communications supported printing and publishing.

Abbreviations

ADB	–	Asian Development Bank
ASEAN+3	–	Association of Southeast Asian Nations plus Japan, the People's Republic of China, and the Republic of Korea
EU	–	European Union
fintech	–	financial technology
GDP	–	gross domestic product
IMF	–	International Monetary Fund
NPL	–	nonperforming loan
PRC	–	People's Republic of China
US	–	United States

Executive Summary

Global financial integration has deepened Asia's global market connections over the past 2 decades. The benefits of greater financial integration include increased and more sophisticated sources of funding, more efficient capital allocation, better governance, higher investment and growth, and risk-sharing. However, between 1990 and the present, the global economy experienced the 1997 Asian financial crisis, the 2008 global financial and economic crisis, the 2009–2011 eurozone sovereign debt and banking crisis (European debt crisis), and an unprecedented easing of monetary policy by advanced economies such as the United States (US), Japan, and the euro area.

A review of the causes, consequences, and policy responses to the Asian financial crisis, global financial crisis, and European debt crisis will help policy makers monitor and evaluate their respective economies for areas of vulnerability. Common elements in these crises would include high leverage in the financial system and asset bubbles of varied nature and force.

To understand the various crises holistically, it would be useful to study the theoretical framework that traces the transmission of financial shocks to the real sector. This falls under the rubric of macrofinancial linkages. The theory can explain how greater financial interconnectedness can amplify financial cycles, which increases the likelihood of financial crises.

At the center of the macrofinancial nexus lies the relationship between asset prices and macroeconomic outcomes. However, the apparent disconnect between asset prices, fundamentals, market volatility, and other phenomena, on the one hand, and the predictions of standard models, on the other, has led many to question the "efficient markets" framework and instead focus on financial market imperfections. These emanate from either the demand side or supply side of finance. In the demand side, changes in borrowers' balance sheets can amplify macroeconomic fluctuations while shocks that emanate from the supply side deal with factors that affect bank lending, bank capital, the leverage cycle, and liquidity conditions.

Ample empirical evidence shows how greater financial interconnectedness in Asia has led to greater vulnerability. Network analysis shows that over time, the network's density has changed substantially before and after crises. Overall, the empirical results show interconnectedness increases during periods of stress, followed by a decrease during recovery phases, with the average strength of linkages growing pre-crisis, before declining significantly.

Meanwhile, given the importance of the liability side as a channel of financial contagion, an empirical investigation tests the contagion effect of an economy using bilateral data on bank claims between economies. The results show the effect of direct and indirect exposures of emerging economies to crisis-affected economies and confirm that these exposures account for the capital outflows from emerging economies.

A panel vector autoregression analysis of the macrofinancial implications of nonperforming loans (NPLs) in emerging Asia offers new insights and significant evidence for the feedback effects of NPLs on real economy and financial variables. The cross-border transmission of the impact of NPLs operates through various channels: (i) cross-border bank lending, (ii) changes in investor confidence, (iii) changes in bank asset (or liability) value due to financial market fluctuations, and (iv) a trade channel where lower growth in high NPL economies translates into lower import demand.

The exchange rate is the most important asset price in the open economy model. Recent theoretical models consider the role of financial variables and valuation effects in studying the linkages between exchange rates and real and financial aggregates. The relatively large share of external debt in US dollars in emerging Asia makes the impact of local currency depreciation ambiguous. This depends on whether the negative effects of the financial channel outweigh the positive effects of the trade channel or vice versa.

Policy responses to reduce financial vulnerability have to consider macrofinancial linkages. They can be categorized into policies carried out domestically, those that require regional cooperation, and those established internationally under the label of the New Financial Regulatory Framework. Domestically, macroprudential policies can be useful in dampening the procyclicality of the financial system. Countercyclical provisions, capital and liquidity buffers, and balance sheet instruments such as leverage ratios and limits on debt-to-income and loan-to-value ratios are good examples. An example of regional cooperation is the Asian Bond Markets Initiative, which helped deepen and strengthen local currency bond markets; its main goal is to channel Asian savings into investment projects located in Asia. Meanwhile, the Financial Stability Board and the Basel III guidelines are the key features of the New Financial Regulatory Framework.

These policies have to be tailored to the needs of individual economies, as the experiences of Cambodia and Mongolia show. Mongolia was subject to an Extended Fund Facility under the auspices of the International Monetary Fund, directed primarily at the adverse effects of quasi-fiscal activities of the Bank of Mongolia. In contrast, Cambodia successfully strengthened its banks by raising minimum capital requirements.

Over the past decade, innovations in financial technology (fintech) have posed additional challenges to global economic stability. In general, technological developments have not yet resulted in any major upheaval in the structure of financial regulation. However, the activities of fintech and "Big Tech" firms can lead traditional financial institutions to take more risks to maintain profitability. Policy makers should be forward looking in this regard and consider innovation offices and regulatory sandboxes.

1 Introduction

Global financial integration has expanded rapidly in the past several decades, driven by changes in policy and advances in technology. Asia has participated extensively in this process. Evidence of deeper integration can be gleaned, for example, from network analysis (Dungey et al. 2017). Empirical results reveal a complex global financial network. Analysis also points to a general deepening of Asia's market connections with the rest of the world—as well as within the region—over the past 2 decades.

The benefits of greater financial integration include increased and more sophisticated sources of funding, more efficient capital allocation, better governance, higher investment and growth, and risk-sharing. The issue has been analyzed from both theoretical and empirical standpoints. However, between 1990 and the present, the global economy experienced the 1997 Asian financial crisis, the 2008 global financial and economic crisis, the 2009–2011 eurozone sovereign debt and banking crisis (European debt crisis), and an unprecedented easing of monetary policy by advanced economies such as the United States, Japan, and the euro area. These turbulent episodes reflect the greater risk that deeper financial integration spawns, and the coronavirus disease (COVID-19) pandemic threatens to expose financial markets to these risks anew.

The Asian financial crisis and global financial crisis overhauled the view of the relationship between macroeconomics and finance—particularly the impact of macrofinancial linkages on the real economy.

This report analyzes the impact of deeper financial integration on economic vulnerability. It also consolidates six background studies[1] that served as inputs to the theme chapter of the 2017 Asian Economic Integration Report entitled "The Era of Financial Interconnectedness: How Can Asia Strengthen Financial Resilience?" (ADB 2017). The theme chapter itself will guide the discussion. The Asian financial crisis, global financial crisis, and European debt crisis can shed light on the relationship between financial integration and economic vulnerability.

Meanwhile, it would also be worthwhile to study the theoretical framework that traces the transmission of financial shocks to the real sector, which falls under the rubric of macrofinancial linkages. The theory can explain how greater financial interconnectedness can amplify financial cycles, which increases the likelihood of financial crises. Financial crises are often preceded by rising asset prices—housing prices, credit, and equity. Crisis impacts can include a substantial fall in credit volume and asset prices, impaired financial intermediation, large-scale balance sheet problems, and a sudden stop in capital flows (particularly in emerging markets). These force public interventions or financial regulatory reforms.

---

[1] These are Buckley, Avgouleas, and Arner (2020); Claessens (2017); Dungey et al. (2017); Park and Shin (2017); Lee and Rosenkranz (2019); and Villafuerte (2017).

Over the past decade, innovations in financial technology (fintech) have further challenged global economic and financial stability. Financial innovation benefits developing economies by providing financial services with the potential to increase market access, the range of product offerings, and convenience, while lowering costs to clients (Financial Stability Board 2019a). However, the heightened competition generated by fintech and Big Tech[2] firms can lead traditional financial institutions to take more risks to maintain profitability. Fintech firms unduly benefit from regulatory arbitrage due to the limited scope of existing regulation (ADB 2019b). Moreover, greater third-party dependencies could have new implications for financial stability. These include services like cloud, digital platforms, and distributed ledger technology, and they involve systemic operational and cybersecurity risks related mainly to unauthorized access to personal data of customers.

The government's response to these challenges can benefit economies in the long run, as crises can be the impetus to much-needed and often difficult reforms—often politically difficult to implement during normal times. Such policies not only address crisis management, but also crisis prevention. Empirical evidence and theory can form the basis for monitoring vulnerabilities and policy recommendations.

---

[2]   Big Tech firms are large companies with established technology platforms, such as Alibaba, Amazon, Google, and eBay. Fintech firms are a broader class of technology firms—many of which are smaller than Big Tech firms—that offer financial services.

2 A Review of Past Crises

While the three crises described in this section are distinctive, they share common causes (e.g., Claessens et al. 2014). These would include high leverage in the financial system and asset price bubbles of varied nature and force. High leverage, particularly of households, is usually accompanied by credit booms which, in turn, are associated with a deterioration of lending standards. The result is the creation of marginal assets viable only while favorable economic conditions persist. The expansion of risky economic activity is often caused by incorrect sequencing of regulatory reforms and financial liberalization. These factors can be related directly to deeper financial integration.

The Asian Financial Crisis

The Asian financial crisis was an important watershed in the economic development of the Asia and Pacific region.

Its four principal causes were the type and extent of indebtedness, financial sector weaknesses, fixed local exchange rates, and a region-wide loss of confidence, which eventually spread to emerging market economies worldwide (Buckley, Avgouleas, and Arner 2020). The crisis was rooted in the nature of foreign borrowing, which created a double maturity and currency mismatch. Much of foreign capital inflows were short-term, i.e., below 1-year maturity, and unhedged. Inadequate prudential supervision and lack of proper regulations allowed these short-term inflows to be invested in long-term domestic projects—many in real estate and unproductive sectors.

Meanwhile, the currency mismatch stemmed from the de facto US dollar peg in place in most Asian economies, including those hardest hit by the crisis. The peg gave borrowers a false sense of security, encouraging them to take on increasing amounts of US dollar debt. In other words, it made domestic financial institutions less cautious about exchange rate risks. Gaps in the financial sector played a crucial role as well. Asian economies lacked the financial market infrastructure, supervision, and regulatory environment to efficiently allocate foreign capital inflows. Liberalizing local financial markets was premature and insufficiently regulated. Weak banking systems, poor corporate governance, and an overall lack of transparency contributed to the vulnerabilities in the region's financial systems.

The crisis originated in Thailand after its economy was made vulnerable by the high volume of foreign capital that poured into the country in the years leading up to the crisis. These capital inflows fueled speculative markets in real estate and stocks alongside heavy domestic consumption. These factors contributed to a growing, unsustainable current account deficit. Authorities tried to defend the value of the Thai baht, but were ultimately forced to devalue the currency in early July 1997.

The large current account deficit in Thailand led to a sharp depreciation of the baht that ultimately led to investor panic.

The sharp currency depreciation transformed vulnerabilities in bank balance sheets caused by the double mismatch problem into weaknesses. A vicious cycle ensued consisting of currency depreciation➜financial vulnerability turning to weakness➜fundamentals contagion➜capital outflow➜currency depreciation. Capital outflows were caused by investor panic that reflected erratic shifts in market expectations, with subsequent regional contagion (McCawley 2017). Indonesia, the Republic of Korea, Malaysia, and the Philippines were dragged into the crisis: financial stress spread to neighboring economies as currency and then banking crises surfaced as the previously large capital inflows to the region slowed or reversed. This reflects their financial interconnectedness because of the common sources of capital inflows. The extent and magnitude of the Asian financial crisis can be traced to vulnerabilities of the currency mismatch in the five countries that were hardest hit, which fueled economic slowdowns in each. In little more than a year, gross domestic product in Indonesia, Malaysia, the Philippines, the Republic of Korea, and Thailand fell a combined 30% (ADB 2017). Banks succumbed to ever-expanding portfolios of nonperforming loans (NPLs). Investment rates plunged. And with several Asian economies in deep recession, spillovers affected trading partners across the region and around the globe.

Asian countries learned painfully that no mechanism existed to provide liquidity of an *appropriate* amount and in a *timely* fashion. Liquidity assistance was eventually provided, but the International Monetary Fund (IMF) drew from its experience in crises in Latin America during the 1980s and the crisis in Mexico in 1994, and prescribed restrictive economic and financial policies as well as structural reforms. Hence, the IMF tool kit was not adjusted in line with the nature of Asian financial crisis that originated from the volatility of capital accounts. The tight policies further curtailed aggregate demand and thus deepened the economic downturn. Consequently, the experience led to a reassessment by the international community of its response to financial crises. Box 1 describes the role of the Asian Development Bank (ADB) during this period.

Among the lessons of the Asian financial crisis were the need to (i) develop long-term currency bond markets as an alternative to bank financing, (ii) enhance the infrastructure of local capital markets, and (iii) undertake prudential regulation and supervision (ADB 2017).

In terms of crisis management, policy makers realized that no international debt workout arrangements were in place to address investor panic. Subsequent calls for reform of the international financial architecture cited the need for codes of good conduct for creditors and sovereign debtors, and collective action clauses in the management of sovereign bonds. For crisis prevention, there was a need to develop long-term local currency sovereign bond markets to avoid future currency and maturity mismatches and provide more stable sources of financing. More broadly, the crisis highlighted the need for local capital markets and to establish mechanisms for adequate macroprudential regulation and supervision. The region gained a shared understanding that the lack of regional capital markets and largely underdeveloped domestic financial systems substantially hindered the channeling of the region's savings into investments within emerging Asia. The crisis proved to be a catalyst for deeper economic and financial integration in Asia, in particular by highlighting the need for financial cooperation for ASEAN+3 finance policy makers.[3]

Given the risks of foreign currency borrowing (and US dollar funding in particular), local and international bank regulators need to maintain the safety and soundness of their domestic banking systems and to look out for excessive capital inflows—specifically those that fund consumption or fuel local asset bubbles rather than contribute to expanding productive capacity. Apart from restrictions on short-term capital flows, national

---

[3]   This comprises the 10 members of the Association of Southeast Asian Nations plus the People's Republic of China; Hong Kong, China; Japan; and the Republic of Korea.

and regional financial safety net measures designed to enhance financial resilience include ensuring adequate levels of foreign currency reserves and the development of regional financial cooperation mechanisms for crisis management (such as the Chiang Mai Initiative Multilateralization [CMIM]). Finally, the Asian financial crisis showed that the timing and sequence of external financial liberalization matters for financial sector development and stability in Asia (Park et al. 2017).

Box 1: ADB's Response during the Asian Financial Crisis

Fortunately, Asian Development Bank (ADB) operational systems had become more flexible during the 1990s. Having evolved into a broad-based development institution, ADB had the staff resources to monitor the situation closely and to liaise with member countries, the International Monetary Fund (IMF), the World Bank, and bilateral donors. ADB was able to contribute to IMF-driven emergency assistance packages financially and by guiding developing member countries toward reforms in the public sector and the financial capital markets. This required detailed work on financial market regulation, governance, and capacity building—all of which consolidated ADB's capacity to provide a broadening range of services to member countries.

Just as important, ADB recognized the need to respond to severe social problems. Unemployment was rising sharply, children were dropping out of school, and malnutrition was rising. In Thailand and Indonesia, ADB programs (such as the health and nutrition sector loan for Indonesia) financed social safety nets to mitigate damage. Under the circumstances, ADB had to set aside normal procedures to respond quickly. Different dimensions of the crisis called for a different focus in each country.

Source: McCawley, P. 2017. The Asian Financial Crisis. In P. McCawley. *Banking on the Future of Asia and the Pacific: 50 Years of the Asian Development Bank*. Manila: Asian Development Bank.

The Global Financial Crisis

The global financial crisis unfolded largely because improperly designed regulatory systems facilitated overinvestment in real estate, financed by increasingly complex, repackaged (and difficult to trace) financial vehicles.

The five principal causes of the global financial crisis were (i) excessive leverage fueled by lax monetary policies, (ii) poorly functioning credit markets that underpriced risk, (iii) a disconnect between regulatory structures and the financial system, (iv) misaligned incentives, and (v) interconnectedness that facilitated the global transmission of systemic risk. Each of these in turn was underpinned by an excessive reliance on quantitative risk management mechanisms (Buckley, Avgouleas, and Arner 2020).

The crisis began as a domestic mortgage crisis in the US which rapidly spread across the world after the failure of Lehman Brothers Holdings, a major financial services company, and the near-failure of American International Group, an insurance conglomerate. Because of the widespread nature of the crisis, international funding markets froze. The liquidity squeeze forced regulators worldwide to recapitalize financial institutions—including those not normally subject to bailouts—and become the lender of last resort for markets. Aside from excessive borrowing and lending, poorly functioning credit markets, misaligned incentives, and a disconnect between regulatory structures and the rapidly integrated and sophisticated financial system, the global financial crisis was also a product of the international transmission of systemic risk.

The crisis underscored how increased financial integration and cross-border financial interlinkages can transmit risk globally, fueled by vulnerabilities and ultimate failure of "systemically important financial institutions." The global financial crisis also exposed the information gap between cross-border institutions and the inability of international and domestic regulatory structures to manage them effectively. In addition, it exposed failures in financial market funding and the lack of prudential supervision. The excessive reliance on quantitative risk management mechanisms exacerbated the principal causes of the global financial crisis—as they proved incapable of dealing with extreme market stress. The immediate government response was to inject massive amounts of capital to rescue systemically important financial institutions. This approach contrasted with the IMF response to the Asian financial crisis, which included very different measures, such as the closure of financial institutions and addressing of distressed assets. Strengthening bank balance sheets and stabilizing financial systems ultimately restored banks' ability to resume lending.

The international Group of Twenty forum and newly created Financial Stability Board[4] established the foundations underlying the new regulatory framework. They were charged with coordinating post-global financial crisis responses and financial regulatory reforms, as well as setting financial standards and monitoring adherence to these standards. These reforms are still being implemented, so their effectiveness cannot yet be fully gauged. Nonetheless, national regulatory practices have diverged recently alongside a reluctance to abide by certain strictures—such as the capital adequacy frameworks set out under Basel III issued in 2010 by the Basel Committee on Banking Supervision.

The breadth and depth of the global financial crisis generated more extensive research on financial interconnectedness and the global transmission of systemic risk.

The major financial policy lessons of the global financial crisis included the need to (i) provide adequate financial supervision and macroprudential regulation, (ii) devise early warning systems to detect and mitigate the buildup of systemic risk, and (iii) design a framework to resolve systemically important financial institutions.

Mechanisms for the early detection, mitigation, and effective resolution of crises and systemically important financial institutions are critical for financial stability and resilience. The inability to prevent and address systemic risk proved to be a crucial limitation of the regulatory architecture prevailing prior to the global financial crisis. Consequently, regulators need to detect and identify risks earlier to mitigate the transmission of systemic risk. Moreover, they need to have the tools and mechanisms to ensure funding markets remain liquid under all market conditions.

More effective financial regulations and macroprudential supervision are critical to mitigating risks associated with complex financial instruments. Improving financial market infrastructure can likewise help contain possible sources of systemic risk (such as establishing central counterparty clearinghouses). Regulatory bodies must possess the tools and mechanisms to assess and manage risks across the financial system, as well as those that aggregate over time.

The absence of an effective resolution mechanism for systemically important financial institutions was a main factor behind the Lehman Brothers collapse and near collapse of the American International Group. A critical regulatory deficiency was the inability to adequately respond to the failure of large financial conglomerates and identify the risks inherent in cross-border interactions and interconnections. Regulatory bodies must have appropriate resolution powers and measures at their disposal to prevent serious financial instability in times of stress. The Asian financial crisis and the global financial crisis more broadly highlighted the need to establish appropriate responses and resolution mechanisms—particularly for domestic or regional systemically important financial institutions. Regional dialogue has helped—especially in the context of executing the ASEAN Banking Integration Framework.

---

[4]   The Financial Stability Board was established after the G20 London summit in April 2009 as a successor to the Financial Stability Forum.

The European Debt Crisis

The European debt crisis evolved as the euro area dealt with weaknesses and failures of banks operating across borders.

Europe represents the most advanced stage of regional financial integration and regulation in the world today. Analysis of the integration of equity and bond markets across European and East Asian financial markets points to the significantly higher level of financial integration in Europe (Calvi 2010). This is because the European Union (EU) has the tightest regional political, economic, and financial structure with the longest history. Moreover, the EU provides by far the richest source of information and experience about regional financial sector policy. The EU can, therefore, provide valuable lessons for Asia and other regions, including negative lessons related to the eurozone sovereign debt and banking sector crisis.

The financial shocks during the global financial crisis spilled over to most developed economies, including EU members. Despite much discussion and work toward establishing a "single financial market," no single EU regulator existed when the global financial crisis erupted. Adequate crisis resolution mechanisms—particularly those dealing with cross-border issues—were unavailable for nearly all EU jurisdictions. The threat of widespread bank failures thus accompanied the near collapse of the region's financial system. The banking crisis eventually gave way to a sovereign debt crisis, triggered by the excessive leverage in the banking systems of countries such as Cyprus, Ireland, and Spain. At the same time, markets became increasingly reluctant to roll over Greek debt, resulting in eventual IMF and EU rescue programs.

The European debt crisis exposed major weaknesses of the euro area's institutional framework and has been compounded by an insufficient policy response. One of the major shortcomings that led to the European dilemma was that monetary unification was not accompanied by an adequate level of financial and macroeconomic cooperation among euro area countries. The crisis exposed many gaps in the EU regional architecture that need to be addressed, including the absence of institutions capable of handling cross-border banking crises. Also, regulatory and institutional features crucial to support financial stability were insufficiently robust or nonexistent. This was particularly relevant for those resolving cross-border financial institutions, deposit guarantee arrangements, and providing regulatory, supervisory, and fiscal arrangements. The severity grew given the tight links between financial institutions operating in a single market—as links amplified the transmission of shocks across market segments.

In response to the European debt crisis, reforms focused on the absence of appropriate regional institutional arrangements.

The European debt crisis (and global financial crisis) underscored a need to revisit existing models of financial market integration—to ensure they had institutions and structures that could underpin financial stability and economic growth. It triggered a wave of regional policy initiatives toward establishing a European banking union—including a new European emergency financial assistance facility, euro area banking supervision, and resolution mechanisms.

Four reforms are worth noting. First, the European Stability Mechanism was established, aimed at providing financial assistance to euro area economies and troubled banks during a crisis. Second, the Single Supervisory Mechanism for euro area banks was organized under the European Central Bank (ECB). An October 2013 Single Supervisory Mechanism Regulation gave the ECB investigatory and supervisory powers to (i) license financial institutions in the European Monetary Union; (ii) monitor compliance with capital, leverage, and liquidity requirements; (iii) supervise financial conglomerates; and (iv) require banks to take remedial action when regulatory capital requirements are breached. Third, EU plans for harmonizing members' resolution laws and introducing integrated resolution structures are being implemented. The Single Resolution Mechanism was established in 2014 to ensure continuity in essential banking operations; to protect depositors, assets, and public funds; and to safeguard overall financial stability. The mechanism should ensure speedy and credible resolution of cross-border failures. Based on the EU's "Single Rulebook", both the Single Supervisory Mechanism and the Single Resolution Mechanism are pillars of the European banking union. And fourth, the development of common EU rulebooks for the single market by the European Supervisory Authorities is under way.

With the failure of previous EU mechanisms to ensure financial market stability, the post-crisis reforms are milestones for greater integration and regionalism. The post-European debt crisis response to further develop and run single market operations underscored the need to improve international and regional coordination.

The European debt crisis highlighted the contagion risks inherent in a highly integrated system—a valuable lesson for Asia as financial integration and interconnectedness deepens. The crisis exposed weaknesses in national regulatory structures—particularly when addressing integrated financial markets. And it made clear the need for harmonized regulatory standards. Those most severely affected by the crisis had to adopt policies based on national circumstances, not necessarily harmonized or conforming to single market policies. This is increasingly relevant for Asia, given the region's heterogeneity in economic size, development, and sociopolitical context.

3 Macrofinancial Linkages and Financial Cycles

The global financial crisis was a stark reminder of how the volatility in asset prices, credit, and capital flows can have a strong impact on the financial position of households, corporations, and sovereign nations.[5]

Economic crises in the past 3 decades, particularly the global financial crisis, have underscored the importance of macrofinancial linkages. Some argue that the crises highlighted the limited knowledge of such linkages. Others claim that the profession has already made substantial progress in understanding them, but that there is too much emphasis on certain approaches and modelling choices. Nevertheless, the absence of a unifying framework to study the two-way interactions between the financial sector and the real economy has limited the practical applications of existing knowledge and impeded the formulation of policies (Claessens and Kose 2018).

This section provides a synopsis of the theoretical and empirical debate, which lays the groundwork for describing the role of macrofinancial linkages in economic crises. It also allows a discussion of the international dimension of these linkages, which is important when accounting for crises contagion. Macrofinancial linkages also provide the basis for relating financial cycles to business cycles.

Limitations of Standard Theory

The global financial crisis underscored the limitations of the theory underlying macrofinancial linkages, which was until that time governed by the "efficient markets" framework.

Macrofinancial linkages deal with the two-way interactions between the real economy and the financial sector. Shocks arising in the real economy can be propagated through financial markets, amplifying business cycles. Conversely, financial markets can be the source of shocks, which, in turn, can lead to more pronounced macroeconomic fluctuations. The global dimensions of these linkages can result in cross-border spillovers through both real and financial channels.

At the center of the macrofinancial nexus lies the relationship between asset prices and macroeconomic outcomes. A long-held view among some academics, market participants, and policy makers is that market forces efficiently set asset prices, which help guide the allocation of resources among competing projects. However, the apparent disconnect between asset prices, fundamentals, market volatility, and other phenomena, on the one hand, and the predictions of standard models, on the other, has led many to question the "efficient markets" framework, especially after the global financial crisis. Nowadays, most experts acknowledge that financial market imperfections are prevalent and often intensify fluctuations in the financial and real sectors.

---

[5]   This section is largely based on Claessens and Kose (2018), Claessens (2017), and ADB (2017).

Financial market imperfections became prominent largely because the links between asset prices and activity differed from the predictions of standard models. These occurred in several ways as reported in the literature. First, asset prices are much more volatile than fundamentals would imply and can at times deviate, or at least appear to do so, from their predicted fundamental values. Moreover, macroeconomic and financial news seem to have an exaggerated effect on asset prices: equities, bonds, and currencies overreact to news about cash flows and other fundamentals.

Second, investment and consumption respond differently to asset prices from what standard models would suggest, with a larger role for "non-price factors" in driving agents' behavior and macroeconomic aggregates. Firm investment reacts less strongly to asset prices than predicted by models, while household consumption reacts more vigorously to changes in asset prices, especially housing prices, than consumption-smoothing models would suggest.

Third, there are limits to the predictive ability of asset prices for real activity. The basic theory implies that asset prices should be good proxies for expected growth as they are forward-looking variables. Equity prices, however, with their (excess) volatility, have a mixed record in forecasting activity. There are also limits to the predictive ability of the bonds yield curve, which depends on the time horizon, country-specific circumstances, and external factors.

Fourth, similar to the domestic context, there are many puzzles involving the international dimensions of asset prices. As is the case for the weak link between equity prices and firms' fundamentals within a country, co-movements in asset prices appear to not (just) reflect commonality in cash flow streams. The observed high correlations across asset prices suggest other channels of transmission, including financial contagion, as suggested by the high volatility of capital flows. The limited international diversification of investment, the so-called home bias, has been hard to reconcile with the predictions of most asset pricing models. The home bias puzzle is the term given to describe the fact that individuals and institutions in most countries hold only modest amounts of foreign equity even if actual returns on various national equity portfolios suggest substantial benefits from international diversification.

Financial Market Imperfections

As stated earlier, financial market imperfections give rise to the deviation of the relationship between asset prices and real economic activity from theoretical predictions.

Financial market imperfections usually emanate from information asymmetries—including principal–agent problems—and difficulties with enforcement of contracts. Such imperfections generally impede access to finance. For example, information asymmetries curtail households' ability to borrow against future labor income, leading to liquidity constraints.

Financial market imperfections can affect macrofinancial linkages through two main mechanisms. The first mechanism largely operates through the demand side of finance, where changes in borrowers' balance sheets can amplify macroeconomic fluctuations. The central idea underlying this channel is best captured by the financial accelerator—an extensively studied propagation mechanism in a wide range of models (Bernanke and Blinder 1988, Kiyotaki and Moore 1997). Shocks to agents' net worth affect their ability to invest or consume, which then means that shocks to commodity or asset prices or to interest rates that work through their balance sheets would have greater real economic outcomes. Endogenous developments in financial markets in response to real or financial shocks can lead to aggregate amplification and propagation of shocks in the real economy.

Shocks that emanate from the supply side deal with factors that affect bank lending, bank capital, the leverage cycle, and liquidity conditions.

The second mechanism, associated with the supply side of finance, emphasizes the importance of balance sheets of banks and other financial institutions in lending and liquidity provision for the real economy. The financial system can be a source of shocks, amplification, and propagation itself, even when on the demand side, no shocks are affecting borrowers. Three channels can be distinguished. The first is the traditional bank lending channel, also referred to as the narrow credit channel. Some borrowers (households, small and medium-sized enterprises) are more bank financing dependent. As shocks affect banks shocks—like bank runs or a surge in nonperforming loans—banks will increase or decrease financing to these classes of borrowers. This has been one of the traditional channels of monetary policy transmission, which has received new attention in light of unconventional monetary policy, such as quantitative easing, conducted by many central banks in advanced countries since the global financial crisis.

Another, but relatively less well-analyzed channel has been the bank capital channel. Balance sheet positions, especially net worth, matter for financial intermediaries, just as is the case for nonfinancial corporations. A deterioration in loan quality or a decline in the value of tradable assets, for example, will adversely affect a bank's capital. When banks have a capital shortfall or some impairment of their balance sheets, they will reduce their provision of credit (Greenwald and Stiglitz 1993, Borio and Zhu 2012).

The third and most recent group of studies on the supply side focuses on the financial system's overall leverage and liquidity. Leverage is defined as the ratio of total assets to shareholder equity. Fluctuations in the leverage of financial institutions relate to changes in asset prices. The global financial crisis showed that leverage could build up to excessive levels during upturns and drop sharply in downturns (Claessens and Kodres 2017). Cycles of growing leverage, ample liquidity, and rising asset prices are readily followed by cycles of deleveraging and liquidity hoarding. These swings in the supply side can have a significant impact on macroeconomic outcomes. A wide range of factors, including balance sheet positions of households, nonfinancial enterprises and financial institutions, interactions between those agents and financial markets, and access to information and ability to process it, can affect asset prices and the supply of external financing (Claessans and Kose 2018).

The macroeconomic implications of financial market imperfections have also been studied in the context of open economy models. Similar to the case of a corporation or household in a closed economy, a country's net worth affects its ability to borrow because of imperfections. Obstfeld and Rogoff (2002) argue that the relevance of imperfections is probably even stronger in an open economy context because contracts are harder to enforce and information asymmetries are greater than is the case in a closed economy. As a result, limited use of output as collateral and limited verifiability of borrowers' credit quality and actions influence access to international finance more than to domestic finance.

Financial and Business Cycles

Financial cycles are longer lasting, more volatile, and more closely related to impending financial crises than business cycles.

Empirical studies that deal with aggregate linkages between the real economy and the financial sector lead to the analysis of financial and business cycles and how they interact. Claessens, Kose, and Terrones (2012) use a comprehensive database for a large sample of advanced economies and emerging market economies over a long period of time to provide a broad empirical characterization of macrofinancial linkages. They report three main results.

First, business cycles are more closely synchronized with credit and house price cycles than with equity price cycles. Second, financial cycles appear to play an important role in determining recessions and recoveries and shaping the features of business cycles more generally. In particular, recessions are more likely to coincide with financial disruptions and recoveries with booms. Third, recessions associated with some forms of financial disruption, notably house price busts, are often longer and deeper than other recessions. Conversely, recoveries associated with rapid growth in credit and house prices tend to be stronger.

Financial cycles—typically related to credit, housing, or equity prices—can stretch over a decade or two, up to twice the typical 6 to 8-year length of business cycles. Financial cycles also have particularly long boom periods and are more volatile (Figure 1). A myriad of factors cause this, including deeper contraction phases relative to business cycles, lengthy downturns in housing prices and credit upturns, and the high coincidence of financial cycle peaks and subsequent financial turmoil. Cycles of credit, housing, and equity prices also tend to reinforce one another. In addition, these cycles coincide globally, underscoring the impact of growing cross-border interconnections.

Figure 1: Average Amplitude of Financial Booms and Busts
(%)

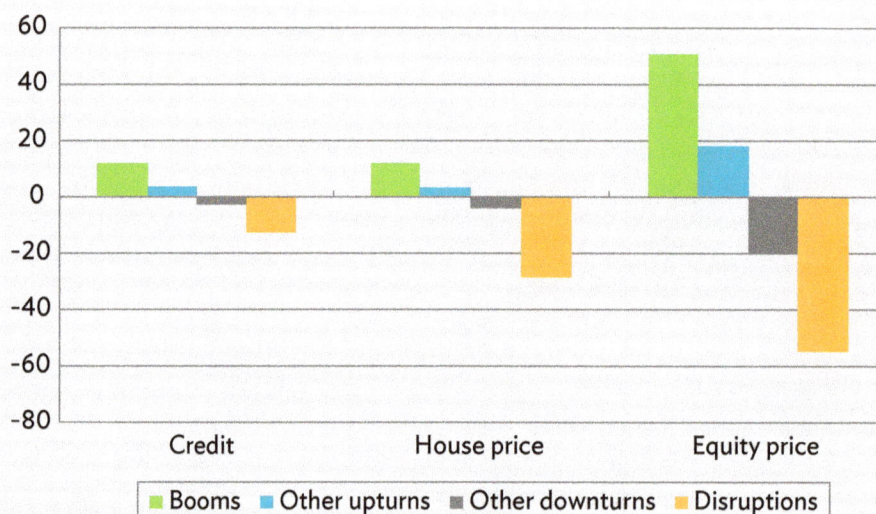

Notes: Figures reflect the average amplitude of upturns and downturns in percent. The amplitude for upturns (downturns) is calculated based on the 1-year change in each respective financial variable after its trough (peak). Booms are the top 25% of upturns calculated by amplitude. Disruptions (crunches, busts, and collapses) are the worst 25% of downturns calculated by amplitude. The dataset includes 21 Organisation for Economic Co-operation and Development (OECD) countries and covers quarterly data from 1960 to 2007 and draws from the International Monetary Fund's International Financial Statistics and OECD (updated to account for data revisions).

Sources: Asian Development Bank (ADB). 2017. *Asian Economic Integration Report 2017: The Era of Financial Interconnectedness, How Can Asia Strengthen Financial Resilience?* Manila; as in Claessens, S. 2017. Financial Cycles and Crises in Asia. Background paper for Asian Economic Integration Report 2017 Theme Chapter on "The Era of Financial Interconnectedness: How Can Asia Strengthen Financial Resilience?" Manuscript.

Meanwhile, the effects of financial cycles spill over to the business cycle, at times with strong interactions. This is evident as recessions coinciding with financial contractions are longer and deeper, and as credit fluctuations are strongly linked to changing output levels (Figure 2). Co-movements between financial and business cycles can similarly occur during periods of economic and financial growth—with financial booms enhancing and lengthening output growth (Figure 3). Thus, the dynamics of the financial cycle need to be better understood—to more effectively detect early signs of financial stress and the buildup of systemic risk. Financial regulation and macroprudential policies have an important role to play in moderating the negative impact of these cycles.

Figure 2: Impact of Financial Disruptions on Recessions

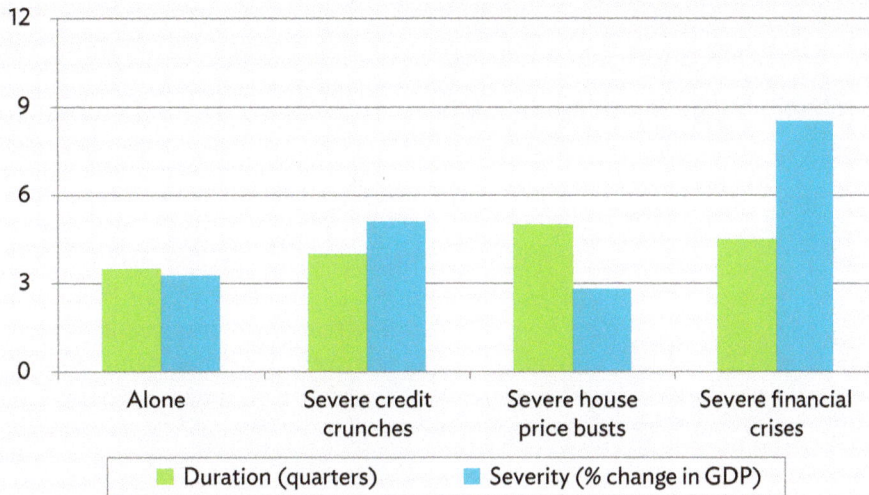

GDP = gross domestic product.

Notes: Severe credit crunches and equity or house price busts are in the top half of all crunch and bust episodes. Duration is the number of quarters from peak to trough in output. The dataset includes 21 Organisation for Economic Co-operation and Development (OECD) countries and covers quarterly data from 1960 to 2007. It draws from the International Monetary Fund's International Financial Statistics and OECD (updated to account for data revisions).

Sources: Asian Development Bank (ADB). 2017. *Asian Economic Integration Report 2017: The Era of Financial Interconnectedness, How Can Asia Strengthen Financial Resilience?* Manila; as in Claessens, S. 2017. Financial Cycles and Crises in Asia. Background paper for Asian Economic Integration Report 2017 Theme Chapter on "The Era of Financial Interconnectedness: How Can Asia Strengthen Financial Resilience?" Manuscript.

Figure 3: Impact of Financial Booms on Expansions

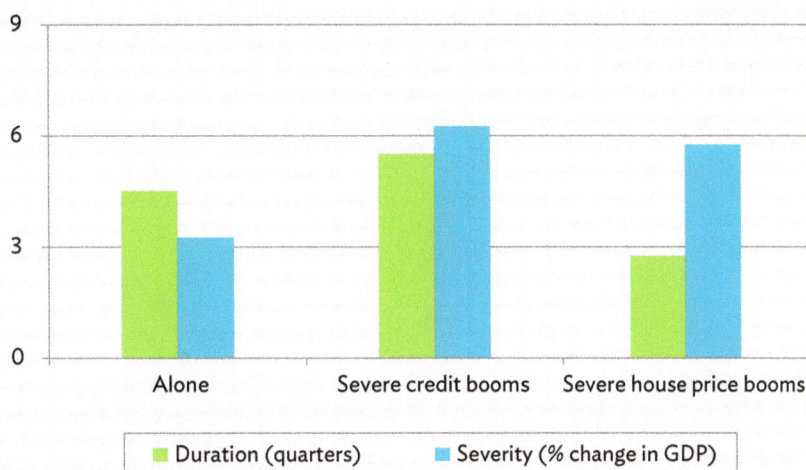

GDP = gross domestic product.

Notes: The dataset includes 21 Organisation for Economic Co-operation and Development (OECD) countries and covers quarterly data from 1960 to 2007. It draws from the International Monetary Fund's International Financial Statistics and OECD (updated to account for data revisions).

Sources: Asian Development Bank (ADB). 2017. *Asian Economic Integration Report 2017: The Era of Financial Interconnectedness, How Can Asia Strengthen Financial Resilience?* Manila; as in Claessens, S. 2017. Financial Cycles and Crises in Asia. Background paper for Asian Economic Integration Report 2017 Theme Chapter on "The Era of Financial Interconnectedness: How Can Asia Strengthen Financial Resilience?" Manuscript.

The deeply interconnected nature of financial systems is underscored by the high degree of synchronization of financial cycles globally.

A global financial cycle—showing commonalities in credit, asset prices, and financial conditions across countries—appears in part driven by financial and economic conditions in major financial centers, such as the euro area, Japan, the United Kingdom, and the US—the G4. US monetary policy, global liquidity conditions (especially US dollars), the strength of G4 banking systems, and global risk aversion all have important implications for the high synchronicity of global capital flows and its financial ramifications for Asia.

The global financial cycle matters for financial stability in emerging economies, with liquidity conditions in advanced economies affecting international capital flow dynamics. Among the lessons from past crises have been the long-lasting destabilizing effects large and volatile capital flows can have on emerging market economies. In an increasingly integrated global financial system, this is even more crucial when designing effective policy responses given more rapid international risk transmission. This amplifies shock propagation and synchronization in the region, potentially undermining financial stability.

Empirical results suggest that monetary policy in advanced economies—in the form of low interest rates, quantitative easing, and market expectations about policy moves—heavily impacts capital inflows to Asia (e.g., Villafuerte 2017). Changes in monetary policy can also trigger increased capital flow volatility. These inflows create upward pressure on asset prices (currencies, equities, and bonds) and increase foreign ownership of local currency securities in target economies, increasing local financial market sensitivity to swings in foreign investor sentiment.

Financial Technology and Financial Development and Stability

Financial innovation offers new ways to reduce financial system frictions by increasing the efficiency, accessibility, and provision of financial services, but there are also concerns over possible risks to regional financial stability.

As fintech firms, Big Tech firms, and markets for third-party services continue to develop, it will be important to continue monitoring specific developments and their financial stability implications. The more important aspects in this area are (i) new providers of bank-like services competing or cooperating with established financial services providers, (ii) provision of financial services by large technology companies, and (iii) reliance on third-party providers for cloud services (FSB 2019b).

Financial innovation has blurred the lines between fintech firms and traditional financial service providers. This potential transition could lead to many financial service providers with greater incentives for risk-taking activities—due to their licenses falling outside the regulatory perimeter. This has implications for balance sheets of banks and can affect bank capital and bank lending.

Adding to the risks presented by fintech activities, fintech regulation remains challenging (ADB 2019b, page 74). This is due to numerous factors. Among these (i) fintech firms benefit from regulatory arbitrage due to the limited scope of existing financial regulation—while fintech firms increasingly diversify reach and essentially provide banking and other financial services, fintech firms have less reporting and regulatory requirements as licenses are subject to less stringent monitoring. It is also due to (ii) limited regulatory experience, resulting in difficulty understanding and assessing fintech's regulatory implications; (iii) resource constraints, especially for emerging and developing economies, which limit adequate responses to fintech risks; and (iv) the focus on domestic financial landscape, which increases risks for cross-border regulatory arbitrage.

4 Evidence of Financial Interconnectedness and Economic Vulnerability in Asia

Greater financial integration is a double-edged sword. As stated in the introduction, financial integration and interconnectedness allow more efficient allocation of financial resources and create greater opportunities for economic growth regionally and/or globally. However, because of the macrofinancial linkages, deeper cross-border financial connections and higher associated volumes of cross-border financial flows can be a source of financial volatility and contagion, in particular, in emerging market economies. Financial market imperfections that work through the supply side are important in this regard.

This section looks at various empirical studies that document the degree of interconnectedness and vulnerability in Asia. The discussion starts with a description of existing vulnerabilities. As with the Asian financial crisis, these vulnerabilities can turn to weaknesses because of the amplification of shocks through macrofinancial linkages.

While Asian equity markets were subdued in 2018, alongside the moderation of global growth and continuation of global trade tensions, the region's portfolio debt investment grew modestly (up 2.6% in outward debt investment and 3.8% inward), portfolio equity investment contracted (a 6.6% decline in outward equity investment and 12.9% inward), and the volume of banking activities reached a record high (up 1.8% for claims and by 2.8% for liabilities). The slowdown in inward equity investment reflected mounting concerns over Asia's uncertain economic outlook, in line with continued trade tensions. The ongoing increase in the region's cross-border banking activities underline the need for monitoring in the event of a reversal of the global liquidity cycle (ADB 2019b).

Asia and the Pacific has become more resilient since the Asian and global financial crises, but substantial challenges remain and new sources of vulnerability have emerged.

Banks remain the biggest source of corporate financing in emerging Asia. While bank credit amounted to 65.3% of gross domestic product (GDP) in 1999, it ballooned in succeeding decades and comprised 127.6% of GDP in 2019. This figure far outstripped stock market capitalization (57.0% of GDP) and corporate bonds (30.0% of GDP) (Figure 4).

Loans and leverage are rising in several economies, raising concerns of unsustainable credit booms. And as credit increases and deviates from its long-run trend (Figure 5), credit gaps remain, if slightly narrowing. Credit growth was high during the pre-global financial crisis period—particularly in Cambodia, the People's Republic of China (PRC), India, Indonesia, the Republic of Korea, the Lao People's Democratic Republic, Myanmar, and Viet Nam. However, others had low credit growth—Hong Kong, China; Japan; Malaysia; Taipei,China; and Thailand. Generally, credit growth has moderated since 2014, the result of a slowdown in net capital inflows—as global push factors grew bearish with the likely increase in the US Federal Fund rates, moderating PRC growth, and low global commodity prices.

The combination of high leverage and slowing economic growth lowered the debt service capacity of many economies, raising the question of debt-at-risk. Corporate and household debt (and leverage) remains a concern for several economies in the region (Figure 6). The PRC's core debt, for instance, rose from 139% of GDP in the

Figure 4: Corporate Financing—Emerging Asia
(% of GDP)

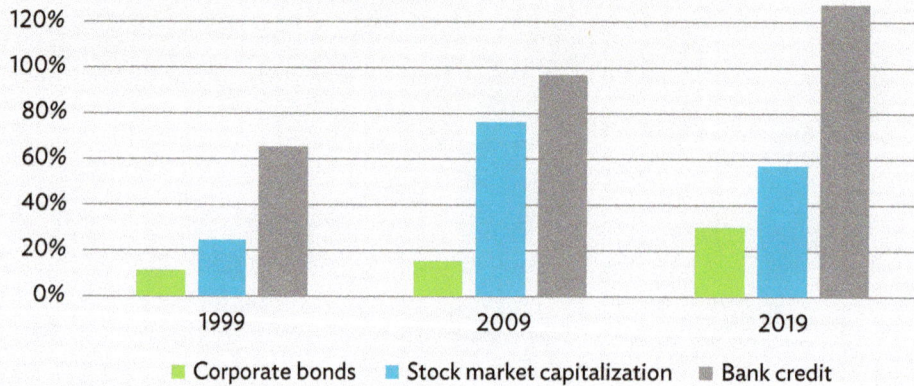

Corporate bonds   Stock market capitalization   Bank credit

GDP = gross domestic product.

Notes:

1. Emerging Asia includes the People's Republic of China, India, Indonesia, the Republic of Korea, Malaysia, the Philippines, Thailand, and Viet Nam.

2. 1999 corporate bond data as of 2000 for the Republic of Korea, Malaysia, the Philippines, Thailand, and Viet Nam. 1999 stock market capitalization data as of 2000 for Viet Nam; as of 2003 for India and the People's Republic of China. 1999 bank credit data as of 2001 for the Philippines; as of 2003 for Indonesia and Thailand.

3. 2009 corporate data as of 2010 for India. 2009 stock market capitalization data as of 2010 for Indonesia.

Sources: *AsianBondsOnline*, CEIC, Haver Analytics, and national sources (accessed 30 April 2020).

Figure 5: Deviation of Credit-to-Gross Domestic Product Ratio from Long-Run Trend
(%)

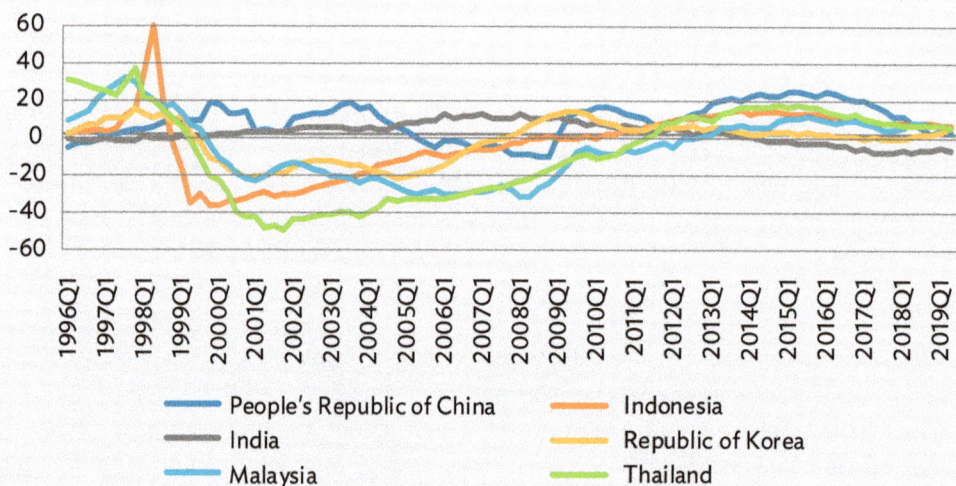

People's Republic of China   Indonesia
India   Republic of Korea
Malaysia   Thailand

GDP = gross domestic product, Q = quarter.

Notes: The credit-to-GDP ratio, published in the Bank for International Settlements database of total credit to the private nonfinancial sector, captures total borrowing from all domestic and foreign sources. In terms of financial instruments, credit covers the core debt, which is here equal to loans and debt securities. A credit-to-GDP gap is defined as the difference between the credit-to-GDP ratio and its long-term trend, in percentage points. The long-term trend is calculated using a one-sided Hodrick-Prescott filter with a smoothing parameter of 400,000.

Source: Bank for International Settlements. https://www.bis.org/ (accessed 31 August 2020).

second quarter of 2009 to 209% of GDP in the second quarter of 2019, mostly due to growing corporate debt. The household debt-to-GDP ratio in the PRC more than doubled from 21% in the second quarter of 2009 to 55% by the second quarter of 2019. The Republic of Korea shows the same pattern—household debt increased from 72% of GDP in the second quarter of 2009 to nearly 93% by the second quarter of 2019. Australia; Hong Kong, China; India; Indonesia; Malaysia; Singapore; and Thailand show similar trends. It has been shown empirically that an increase in the household debt-to-GDP ratio predicts lower GDP growth and higher unemployment in the medium run.[6] Hence, these ratios could prove unsustainable should interest rates rise sharply—from rapid US monetary policy normalization, for example.

Figure 6: Credit to Private Nonfinancial Sector—Selected Asian Economies

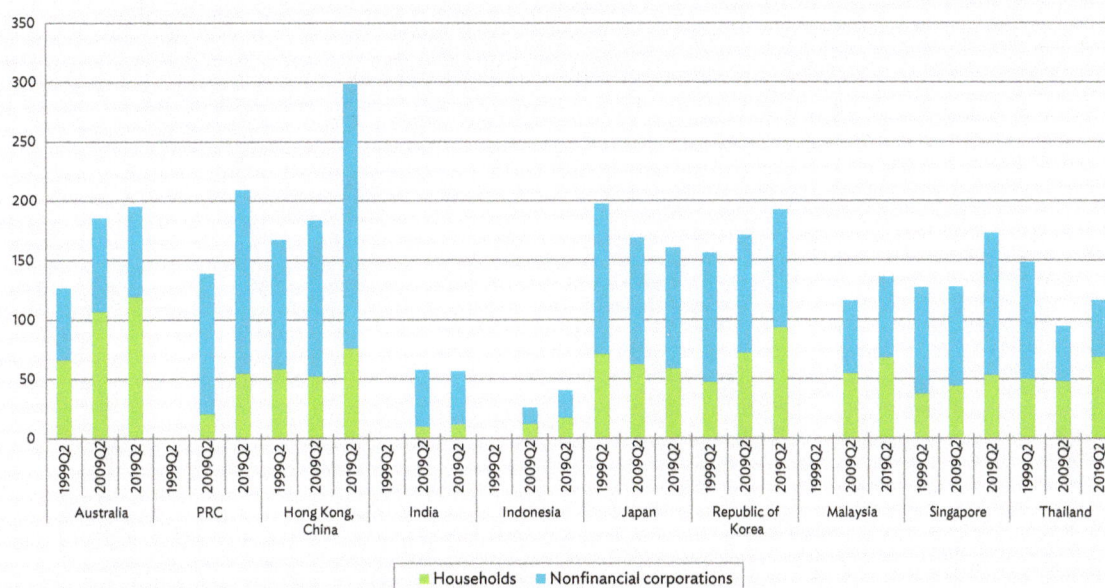

PRC = People's Republic of China, Q = quarter.

Notes: Credit covers core debt, equal to loans plus debt securities, and is provided by domestic banks, all other sectors of the economy and nonresidents. Nonfinancial corporations include both private-owned and public-owned corporations; households include households and non-profit institutions serving households.

Source: Bank for International Settlements. https://www.bis.org/ (accessed 31 January 2020).

---

[6]   Mian, Sufi and Verner (2017), as cited by ADB (2017).

Asia's Financial Sector Network

Network analysis improves the understanding of how financial stress transmits between markets, helping policy makers deal with financial distress.

Since the late-1990s, international financial crises have highlighted the advantage of viewing the global financial system as a network of economies, where cross-border financial linkages play a fundamental role in the spread of systemic risk. Daily equity market returns (in local currencies) from 42 markets around the world (15 from Asia) are used to analyze the changing nature of Asia's financial network for six key periods over the past 20 years. ADB (2017) and Dungey et al. (2017) describe the methodology and results (summarized in Box 2).

The empirical analysis is conducted to effectively model the changing network of financial markets within and between Asia and the rest of the world to capture its evolution through six time periods over the last 2 decades—before, during, and after the Asian financial crisis and global financial crisis, respectively. For each period, the direction of financial links between markets, the relative significance of those links, and their strength is examined. It provides a comprehensive overview of Asia's financial network over time. The network structure allows an examination of the possible buildup of systemic risks within the network and identifies channels of contagion arising from financial market interconnectedness and cross-border financial linkages.

Box 2: The Evolution of Asia's Financial Sector Network

Network analysis is conducted on daily equity market returns—with a particular focus on financial indices—from 42 markets around the world (15 from Asia) to assess the changing nature of Asia's financial networks for six key periods during 1995–2019. The six phases correspond to the periods before, during, and after the 1997–1998 Asian financial crisis and 2008–2009 global financial crisis.

The analysis employs a vector autoregression model to examine the existence and strength of links between equity markets. Nested Granger causality tests are also employed to limit existing links to those with significant Granger causality (i.e., if one equity market [or node] Granger causes another, then the link is recognized as existing in the network).

The box figure maps out the evolution of financial networks over 2 decades. In the pre-crisis to crisis period, the number of significant or strong links increases. Crisis periods then see an increase in the number of linkages, but a decline in their average strength (i.e., the number of weaker connections rises as strong connections decline). Post-crisis periods then see a decline in both the number and strength of linkages. Crisis periods thus see a rising degree of connectedness while the ensuing recovery periods see a decreasing degree of connectedness.

The number of inward and outward linkages from the People's Republic of China increased in the pre-Asian financial crisis period to post-global financial crisis period. Outward and inward linkages to Hong Kong, China increased slightly and both inward and outward linkages grew dramatically in Singapore. These findings support the role of these economies as gateways for connecting Asia's markets to the rest of the world, underlining their financial intermediary role for the region.

Overall, the empirical analysis highlights how interconnectedness increases during periods of financial stress and declines during recovery phases as the average strength of linkages rises in the pre-crisis period before decreasing significantly. The analysis points to a general deepening of Asia's market connections with the rest of the world—and within the region—over the past 2 decades. This suggests the growing internationalization and interconnectedness of Asia's markets.

continued on next page

Box 2 *continued*

Evolution of Weighted Networks

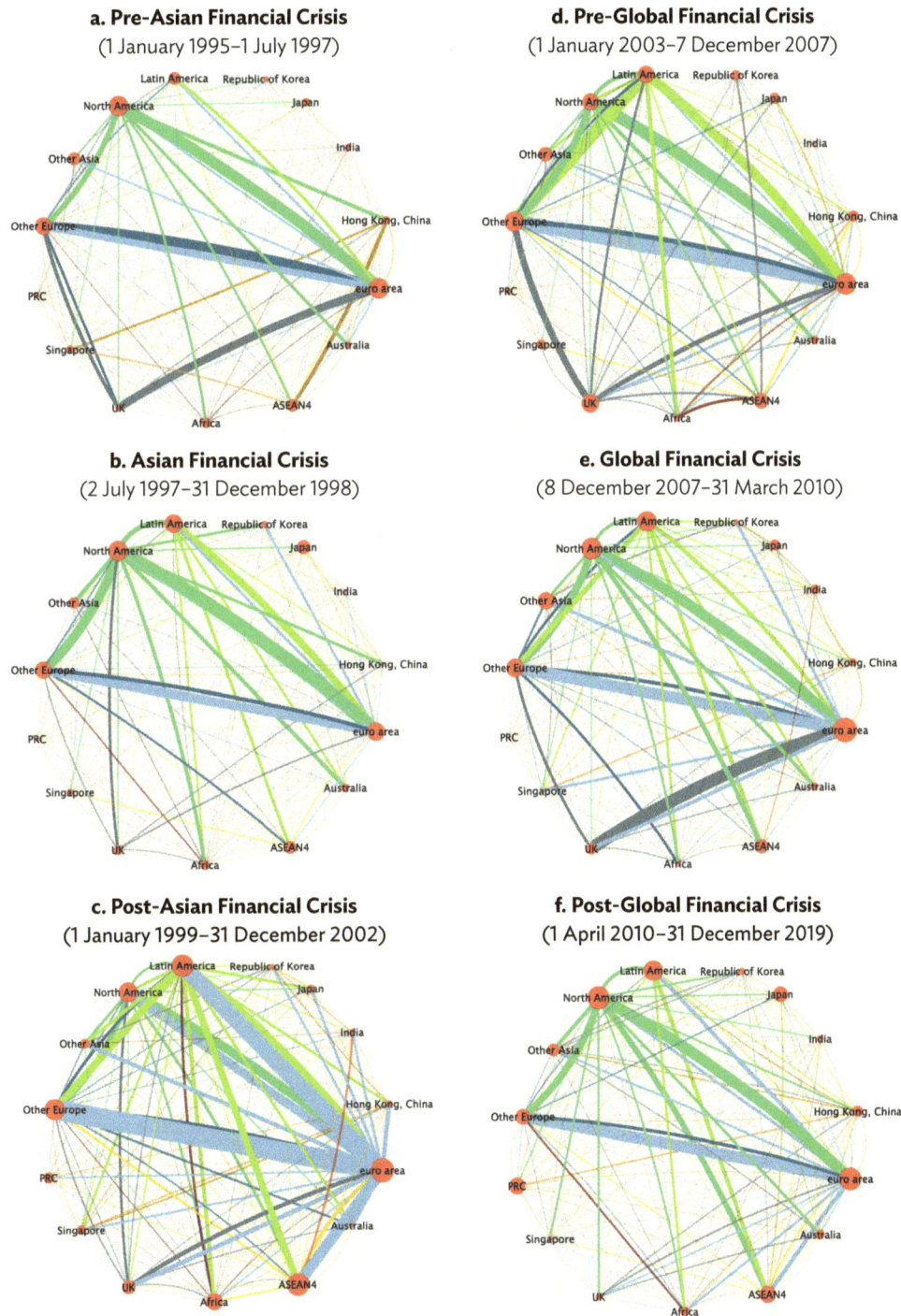

a. Pre-Asian Financial Crisis
(1 January 1995–1 July 1997)

d. Pre-Global Financial Crisis
(1 January 2003–7 December 2007)

b. Asian Financial Crisis
(2 July 1997–31 December 1998)

e. Global Financial Crisis
(8 December 2007–31 March 2010)

c. Post-Asian Financial Crisis
(1 January 1999–31 December 2002)

f. Post-Global Financial Crisis
(1 April 2010–31 December 2019)

ASEAN4 = Association of Southeast Asian Nations (Indonesia, Malaysia, the Philippines, and Thailand); PRC = People's Republic of China; UK = United Kingdom.

Notes: The figure displays the returns-based network of 15 equity markets and regional groupings from from 1 January 1995 to 30 December 2019. Edges were calculated using bivariate Granger causality tests between markets at the 5% level of significance. The thickness of the lines indicates the average relative strength of each link. The size of the nodes increases with the number of outward links of each respective market (or regional grouping).

Sources: Asian Development Bank (ADB). 2017. *Asian Economic Integration Report 2017: The Era of Financial Interconnectedness, How Can Asia Strengthen Financial Resilience?* Manila; calculations updated using data from Bloomberg (accessed 28 February 2020), MSCI and CEIC (both accessed September 2020); and methodology based on Dungey, M. et al. 2017. The Changing Network of Financial Market Linkages: The Asian Experience. Background paper for Asian Economic Integration Report 2017 Theme Chapter on "The Era of Financial Interconnectedness: How Can Asia Strengthen Financial Resilience?" Manuscript.

The advantage of network analysis lies in its ability to better understand the mechanisms underlying the transmission of financial stress between markets, to help identify and monitor network nodes that act as critical links between regions and can, therefore, facilitate the transmission of shocks. More generally, it can help authorities design appropriate policy responses and targeted interventions to promote financial stability and resilience. The following are the salient points of network analysis:

(i)   Empirical results reveal a complex global financial network, highlighting the high degree of financial market interconnectedness. The complexity of the relationships between nodes is evident as there are 1,722 possible connections between nodes. The markets involved are highly interconnected, though some nodes are relatively isolated. The diagram in Box 2 reflects the relatively strong significance of the relationships between European markets in the sample, particularly euro area members. Financial interconnectedness within Asian economies is also visible.

(ii) Tracking the development of the network over time shows that its density has changed substantially before and after crises. Overall, the empirical results show interconnectedness increases during periods of stress, then decreases during recovery phases, with the average strength of linkages growing pre-crisis before declining significantly. Notably, the strength of market connections change from very tight to loose, with the number of weak links growing and the number of strong links decreasing.

(iii) The analysis also suggests a general deepening of Asia's market connections with the rest of the world—as well as within the region—over the past 2 decades.

(iv) The analysis shows the evolution and complexity of expanding financial networks and highlights a growing internationalization and interconnectedness of Asian financial markets. It empirically illustrates the nature of the global and regional financial network, embedding the direction, statistical significance, and strength of interlinkages into a single framework. The trend is associated with shared risks and vulnerabilities, which underscores the need for coordinated action in designing and structuring policies to make the region's financial systems more resilient. As past crises have shown, economies cannot safeguard financial stability alone. Rather, national policies need to be supplemented regionally to make Asia more resilient.

Global Financial Interconnectedness of the Banking Sector

The liability-side exposure of domestic banks to foreign banks is another source of financial market imperfection that generates supply-side vulnerability.

Recent studies look at possible contagion through domestic banks' liability-side exposure to foreign banks during the global financial crisis (Park and Shin 2017, Park and Shin 2018, Shim and Shin 2018). Given the importance of the liability side as a channel of financial contagion, an empirical investigation tests the contagion effect of an economy using bilateral data on bank claims between economies. The goal is to empirically measure the effect of direct and indirect exposures of emerging economies to crisis-affected economies and to test whether these exposures can account for the capital outflows from emerging economies. The complete methodology and results are reported in Park and Shin (2017) as summarized in Box 3.

An emerging economy's direct and indirect exposures on the liability side to crisis-affected banks in advanced economies can explain the capital outflows experienced during the global financial crisis. The results reveal that both direct and indirect exposures to crisis-affected economies play an important role in explaining the capital outflows experienced by emerging market economies during the global financial crisis. These findings highlight the importance of the banking channel for financial distress transmitted from advanced lending economies to borrowing emerging economies.

Box 3: Assessing the Effects of Banking Exposures to Crisis-Affected Countries during the Global Financial Crisis

Analysis of bilateral cross-border data on bank claims between economies suggests that emerging market economies most affected by contagion during the global financial crisis were borrowing from advanced economies experiencing a credit crunch. The analysis utilizes consolidated claims of internationally active banks from 27 Bank for International Settlements reporting economies and 62 counterparty emerging economies. To gauge the extent of exposure of an emerging economy's liability side to borrowing from crisis economies, two indicators are constructed:

$$DE_{i,t}^f = \sum_{j \in C_t} share_{ij,t}^f , \ share_{ij,t}^f = \frac{fc_{ijt}}{\sum_{k=1}^N fc_{ikt}}$$
$$IDE_{i,t}^f = \sum_j share_{ij,t}^f \cdot DE_{j,t}^f$$

Direct exposure of foreign claims on an emerging economy i at time t to banks in crisis economies, denoted by $DE_{i,t}^f$, is measured by the sum of shares of foreign claims held by all economies that experienced crises. However, the direct measure alone cannot fully capture an economy's exposure to crisis-affected economies, because it does not consider the economy's exposure to all other economies not directly hit by the crisis, but similarly exposed to crisis-affected economies—therefore facing indirect liquidity problems. Consequently, an indirect exposure of foreign claims of an emerging economy i at time t, $IDE_{i,t}^f$, is defined accordingly.

The results of the analysis show that the coefficients of direct exposure of the banking sector are positive and statistically significant, regardless of whether indirect exposure is added, and whether economy-specific control variables are included (see table).

Overall, the findings underline that both direct and indirect exposures to crisis-affected economies drive capital outflows experienced by emerging market economies during the global financial crisis. The analysis underscores the importance of the banking channel for financial distress transmitted from advanced lending economies to borrowing emerging economies.

Impact of Direct and Indirect Banking Exposures to the Crisis-Affected Countries on Capital Outflows During the Global Financial Crisis

VARIABLES	(1) Outflow	(2) Outflow	(3) Outflow	(4) Outflow
Direct exposure of banking sector	0.257***	0.228**	0.282***	0.253***
	[0.075]	[0.085]	[0.078]	[0.086]
Indirect exposure of banking sector			0.722**	0.359
			[0.285]	[0.269]

*** = significant at 1%, ** = significant at 5%, * = significant at 10%, GDP = gross domestic product.

Notes: The dependent variable is the rate of capital outflows from each emerging economy during the global financial crisis. Measures of direct and indirect exposures are calculated using cross-border claims on the banking sector based on locational banking statistics. Additional non-reported control variables include: an increase in current account deficit from 2004 to 2007; the average change in real exchange rate from 2003 to 2007 (in %); an increase in the credit-to-GDP ratio from 2004 to 2007; annual GDP growth for 2007 (%); inflation rate for 2007; Chinn-Ito Index for 2007; and S&P Sovereign Local Currency Credit Rating for 2007. See Shin and Park (2017) for more detailed results and data descriptions. Numbers in brackets are robust standard errors.

Source: Park, C. Y. and K. Shin. 2017. A Contagion through Exposure to Foreign Banks during the Global Financial Crisis. *ADB Economics Working Paper Series*. No. 516. Manila: Asian Development Bank.

This empirical exercise shows that shocks in advanced economies are transmitted to emerging economies as the credit crunch experienced by troubled banks, in turn, triggers a run on banks and other entities in emerging economies. The findings underscore the significance of the degree of an economy's direct and indirect exposures through the banking sector to crisis-affected countries as an important determinant of capital outflows. Hence, these findings suggest that the global banking network of aggregate cross-border lending can be a channel for a global liquidity crunch that can spread financial shocks globally. This liquidity issue of creditor banks can be particularly problematic for emerging market economies, as they rely heavily on foreign borrowing denominated in foreign currency.

The findings underscore the need for Asia's emerging economies and the region generally to monitor global conditions affecting their external liability side; and ensure adequate foreign currency liquidity coverage. These findings are highly relevant for policy makers—as they support the idea that cross-border bank lending can serve as an avenue for transmitting global liquidity problems from creditor to borrower economies. They highlight an important channel of contagion and financial vulnerability linked to financial integration and financial interconnectedness.

Macrofinancial Impacts of Nonperforming Loans and Financial Spillovers across Asia

Rising nonperforming loans (NPLs) also affect bank balance sheets, heightening possible macrofinancial linkages that may undermine financial stability.

NPL ratios have recently begun to rise in several developing Asian economies—an emerging concern due to macrofinancial feedback effects. NPL ratios in Asia have been trending downward since the Asian financial crisis—particularly in Southeast Asia, where NPL ratios were 3% or below in 2016 (Table 1). This contrasts starkly with skyrocketing NPL ratios immediately following the crisis in 1999, when they were well above 30% of all loans in Indonesia and Thailand, 29% in the PRC, and over 10% in India, Malaysia, and the Philippines. The improved bank asset quality has been attributed to stronger growth in nominal incomes and credit, increased financial inclusion, and better supervision of bank credit risk management and underwriting.

However, global headwinds and moderating growth in the PRC in recent years exerted downward pressure on the region's economic conditions. Coupled with greater financial volatility following the start of US monetary policy tightening and financial spillovers from the PRC, bank balance sheets have deteriorated, causing a buildup of NPLs in the region. The unfolding COVID-19 pandemic may also result in increasing corporate defaults and, hence, increasing NPLs. A large sustained NPL buildup could damage the financial sector and, likewise, lead to a reduction in credit supply and slow overall economic activity. Multiple studies establish a link between deteriorating macroeconomic conditions (as captured by rising unemployment, slower growth, or falling asset prices) and unfavorable financial conditions (such as debt service problems or mounting distressed assets on bank balance sheets).

Increasing NPL levels reflect weak macroeconomic conditions and excess leverage; and they have harmful feedback effects on the overall economy. However, very few Asian studies model NPLs and their macrofinancial feedback effects. Meanwhile, few have attempted to control for structural changes such as those relating to the Asian financial crisis or global financial crisis. Therefore, a panel vector autoregression (PVAR) analysis of macrofinancial implications of NPLs in emerging Asia offers new insights and significant evidence for the feedback effects of NPLs on real economy and financial variables. The complete study is reported in Lee and Rosenkranz (2019) and is summarized in Box 4. These effects are bidirectional—as macroeconomic conditions impact financial indicators (such as NPLs) and financial conditions in turn affect macroeconomic indicators.

Table 1: Bank Nonperforming Loans
(% of gross loans)

Economy	1997	1998	1999	2000	2001	2002	2003	2004	2005	2006	2007	2008	2009	2010	2011	2012	2013	2014	2015	2016	2017	2018	2019
Central Asia																							
Afghanistan														49.9	4.7	5.0	4.9	7.8	12.1	11.1	12.2	8.9	
Armenia		6.0	8.0	17.5	24.4	9.9	5.4	2.1	2.0	2.4	2.4	4.3	4.9	3.0	3.4	3.7	4.5	7.0	8.0	6.7	5.4	4.8	5.1
Azerbaijan						28.0	21.5	15.1	9.5	7.2				3.5	4.7	6.0	5.7	4.5	4.4	5.3	13.8	12.2	
Kazakhstan						11.9	8.4	4.3	3.3	2.4	2.7	7.1	18.9	20.9	20.7	19.4	19.5	12.4	8.0	6.7	9.3	7.4	8.1
Kyrgyz Republic		10.1	30.9	30.9	13.4	13.3	11.2	8.0		6.2	3.6	5.3	8.2	14.8	9.4	6.6	5.1	4.2	6.7	8.5	7.4	7.3	7.7
Tajikistan				5.2	3.0	5.1	5.2	3.6	3.3	1.1	0.7	2.3	44.3	7.6	6.8	6.4	8.6	11.6	17.2	26.6	21.6	21.2	
East Asia																							
Korea, Republic of					2.8	1.9	2	1.6	1	0.7	0.6	0.9	0.8	1.1	0.9	1	1.2	1	1	1.1	0.9	0.7	0.6
Mongolia		31.0	50.5	21.9	6.7	5.1	4.8	6.4	5.8	4.9	3.3	7.2	17.4	11.5	5.8	4.2	5.3	5.0	7.4	8.5	8.5	10.4	10.1
PRC	19.7		28.5	22.4	29.8	26.0	20.4	13.2	8.6	7.1	6.2	2.4	1.6	1.1	1.0	1.0	1.0	1.2	1.7	1.7	1.7	1.8	1.9
South Asia																							
Bangladesh		40.7	41.1	34.9	31.5	28.1	22.1	17.5	13.2	12.8	14.5				5.8	9.7	8.6	9.4	8.4	8.9	8.9	9.9	8.9
India	14.4	14.7	12.8	11.5	10.4	9.1	7.2	4.9	3.3	2.5	2.3	2.5	2.3	2.2	2.7	3.4	4.0	4.4	5.9	9.2	10.0	9.5	9.2
Maldives																20.9	17.6	17.5	14.1	10.6	10.5	8.9	9.4
Pakistan	24.0	23.0	26.0	24.0	23.0	22.0	17.0	12.0	9.0	7.3	7.4	9.1	12.2	14.8	16.2	14.5	13.0	12.3	11.4	10.1	8.4	8.0	8.6
Southeast Asia																							
Cambodia	7.2	16.2	14.5	12.4	8.4	14.8	13.9	10.3	7.8	9.9	3.4	3.7	4.8	3.1	2.3	2.2	2.3	1.6	1.6	2.1	2.1	2.0	1.6
Indonesia		48.6	32.9	34.4	31.9	24.0	6.8	4.5	7.3	5.9	4.0	3.2	3.3	2.5	2.1	1.8	1.7	2.1	2.4	2.9	2.6	2.3	2.4
Malaysia	4.1	18.6	16.6	15.4	17.8	15.9	13.9	11.7	9.4	8.5	6.5	4.8	3.6	3.4	2.7	2.0	1.9	1.7	1.6	1.6	1.6	1.5	1.5
Philippines	4.7	12.4	14.6	24.0	27.7	14.6	16.1	14.4	10.0	7.5	5.8	4.6	3.5	3.4	2.6	2.2	2.4	2.0	1.9	1.7	1.6	1.7	2.0
Thailand	42.9	38.6		17.7	11.5	16.5	13.5	11.9	9.1	7.8	7.6	5.6	5.2	3.9	2.9	2.4	2.3	2.3	2.7	3.0	3.1	3.1	3.1

PRC = People's Republic of China.

Notes: White cells denote nonperforming loan ratio less than 5%, yellow between 5% and 10%, and orange higher than 10%. Blank cells mean data is not available.

Sources: ADB calculations using data from Bank of Mongolia; CEIC Database; International Monetary Fund Financial Soundness Indicators. https://data.imf.org/; and World Bank. World Development Indicators. http://databank.worldbank.org/data/reports.aspx?source=world-development-indicators (accessed 30 September 2020).

Box 4: Assessing the Determinants and Macrofinancial Feedback Effects of Nonperforming Loans in Asia

To investigate nonperforming loans (NPLs) in emerging Asia from 1994 to 2014, a dynamic panel data model is estimated to examine the determinants of NPLs and a panel vector autoregression (PVAR) model is employed to analyze the feedback effects of a rise in NPLs.

The results of the dynamic panel data model across all specifications underline that both macroeconomic indicators and bank-level variables are important in explaining the evolution of banks' NPL ratio. The real gross domestic product (GDP) growth rate, change in unemployment rate, and inflation rate have considerable effect on NPLs. An economic slowdown raises unemployment and hampers debt servicing capacity, prompting a rise in NPLs. Higher inflation can similarly hurt debt servicing capacity as it weakens real income when wages are sticky. The VIX, exchange rate, and the Asian financial crisis dummy also have an important impact on the evolution of NPLs across banks in emerging Asia as greater global risk aversion and tighter financing conditions exacerbate a surge in distressed assets. Bank-specific factors have a statistically significant, though relatively small, effect on the buildup of credit risk. In particular, a lower equity-to-asset ratio, signifying lower capital, is associated with higher NPLs. The loans-to-deposit ratio—a measure of bank liquidity—and past excessive lending, as captured by the lagged loans growth, are similarly associated with an increase in credit risk. On the other hand, increasing return on equity, signifying higher bank profitability, reduces NPLs.

The PVAR model is estimated as follows:

$$Y_{i,t} = \Pi_0 + \sum_{j=1}^{n} \Pi_j Y_{i,t-j} + \varepsilon_{i,t},$$

$$\varepsilon_{i,t} = u_i + e_{i,t}$$

where $Y_{i,t}$ is the vector of endogenous variables, $\varepsilon_{i,t}$ is the composite error term consisting of the economy fixed effects (u_i) and idiosyncratic errors ($e_{i,t}$). The baseline specification consists of four endogenous variables— $npl r_{i,t}$, $\Delta loans_{i,t}$, $unemp_{i,t}$, and $policyrate_{i,t}$—where subscripts i denotes economy i and t denotes year t.

The results of the PVAR analysis illustrate how a buildup of NPLs can affect the real sector of the economy and spill over through macrofinancial feedback effects. In particular, an increase in NPLs leads to a reduction in credit supply, a rise in unemployment, and a slowdown in overall economic activity (see figure). A one standard deviation shock in the NPL ratio would trigger a 0.18 percentage point contraction in GDP growth rate, approximately 3.61 percentage point decline in loan growth rate, and 0.21 percentage point increase in unemployment after a year. The corresponding figures over 3 years are 0.1, 1.5., and 0.1 percentage points. The results are, moreover, bidirectional as macroeconomic factors can simultaneously prompt changes in the NPL ratio. Greater GDP growth and credit supply decrease the NPL ratio, while tighter monetary policy and rising unemployment increase the NPL ratio.

Estimated Impulse Response Functions to a Shock in the Nonperforming Loan Ratio

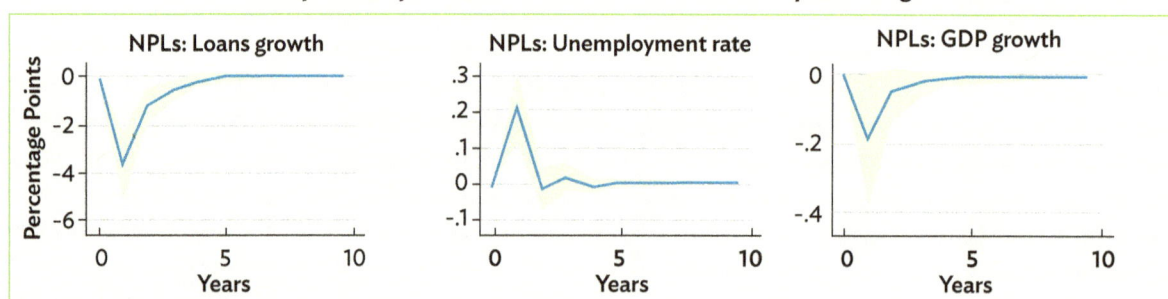

GDP = gross domestic product, NPL = nonperforming loan.

Notes: The figures correspond to impulse responses to a one standard deviation shock in the NPL ratio. By magnitude, a one standard deviation shock in the NPL ratio would trigger a 0.18 percentage point contraction in GDP growth rate, approximately 3.61 percentage point decline in loan growth rate, and 0.21 percentage point increase in unemployment after a year. 95% confidence intervals are generated by 5,000 Monte Carlo draws. Empirical results have been derived using Stata 13 software.

Source: Lee, J. and P. Rosenkranz. 2019. Nonperforming Loans in Asia: Determinants and Macrofinancial Linkages. *ADB Economics Working Paper Series*. No. 574. Manila: Asian Development Bank.

The macrofinancial impact of NPLs may spill over to other economies, transmitted through various channels. In an increasingly integrated global financial system, financial shocks can be transmitted across borders with greater speed and frequency. The cross-border transmission of the impact of NPLs operates through various channels: (i) cross-border bank lending, (ii) changes in investor confidence, (iii) changes in bank asset (or liability) value due to financial market fluctuations, and (iv) a trade channel where lower growth in high NPL economies translates into lower import demand. Through these, increasing NPL levels could (i) undermine the flow of cross-border lending, (ii) damage market sentiment of the region, (iii) have negative wealth effects, and (iv) lead to a deterioration in affected countries' macroeconomic conditions, lowering import demand for others' exports (Martin 2017).

Broadly, the cross-border and systemic implication of NPLs underscores the need for policy makers to swiftly and effectively manage and respond to a buildup of distressed assets. The national and regional mechanisms underlying distressed asset resolution—in particular NPLs—are important for safeguarding financial stability. While it is critical to establish and strengthen national resolution mechanisms, regional cooperation can help advance more effective strategies for identifying and implementing national NPL resolution mechanisms and developing distressed asset markets.

The Exchange Rate and Influence of United States Dollar Funding Conditions

Exchange rate volatility remains an important channel for macrofinancial linkages, but the relevant relationships have become complex, with one factor being the amount of US dollar funding in the economy.

The exchange rate is the most important asset price in the open economy model. The linkages between exchange rates and macroeconomic outcomes are also multidimensional. Many models look at how exchange rates are endogenously related to macroeconomic variables and how these relationships are affected by a variety of factors, including the heterogeneity of economic sectors, economies of scale, imperfect competition, the type of exchange rate regime, country-specific elements, and time horizons.

Recent theoretical models employ richer environments, including a consideration of the role of financial variables and valuation effects in developing a better understanding of the linkages between exchange rates and real and financial aggregates (Tille 2008, Tille and van Wincoop 2014). These studies find evidence that balance sheet and valuation effects appear to be important in driving exchange rates and, in turn, real variables. Meanwhile, some of the links between exchange rates and macroeconomic outcomes remain uncertain, including with respect to the effects of devaluations on investment and output (Claessens and Kose 2018).

A large portion of foreign currency-denominated external debt in emerging Asia is in US dollars. In the first quarter of 2017, 79% of outstanding international debt securities in Asia's major emerging economies was denominated in US dollars. Generally, the ratio of outstanding US dollar-denominated international debt securities to total international debt securities for these economies has increased over time (Figure 7). While the share of dollar-denominated debt securities has fallen moderately since the global financial crisis, there has been an upward trend since the pre-Asian financial crisis period. A high concentration of foreign debt in US dollars deepens an economy's exposure to dollar liquidity risks and more general susceptibility to external shocks.

Figure 7: United States Dollar-Denominated International Debt Securities
(% of external debt)

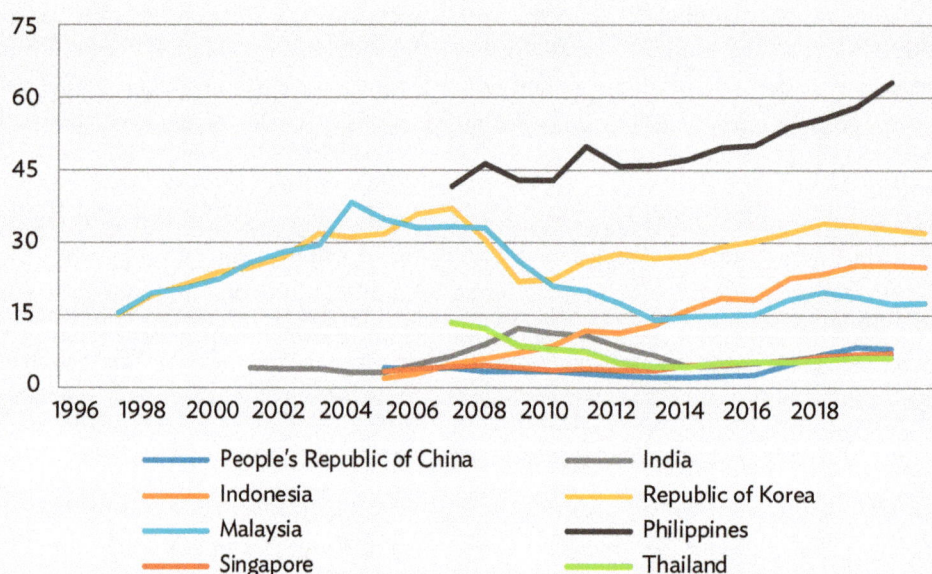

Source: ADB. 2019a. *Asian Development Outlook 2019: Strengthening Disaster Resilience* (April). Manila.

The ambiguous effects of a currency depreciation can, therefore, be traced to deeper financial integration, combined with the dominant role of the US dollar. In theory, the exchange rate may affect domestic financial conditions positively through the trade channel and negatively through the financial channel. In the trade channel, currency depreciation improves international competitiveness, which boosts net exports and eventually improves the current account, which loosens domestic financial conditions. However, currency depreciation can also work through the financial channel by inflating the size of foreign currency denominated debt, tightening domestic financial conditions, and worsening the economy's balance sheet. Depending on which of the two channels dominates, the effect of exchange rates on domestic financial conditions can vary across economies.

Empirical evidence shows the significant impact of a change in bilateral US dollar exchange rates on sovereign bond spreads in selected emerging Asian economies with important implications for their financial conditions. The empirical work is reported in Lee, Rosenkranz, and Pham (2019) and summarized in Box 5. Generally, an appreciation of domestic currency against the US dollar improves the country's balance sheet capacity— decreasing the value of dollar-denominated liabilities relative to assets. Policy makers need to monitor this interplay between the bilateral exchange rate and local financial market conditions. Furthermore, COVID-19 exposes Asian banks' vulnerability to US dollar funding conditions anew, as discussed in ADB (2020a).

The effect of monetary and macroprudential policies on exchange rate movements must be considered.

Measures to minimize the influence of adverse external conditions on domestic financial systems are outlined in ADB (2019a). Ensuring domestic financial stability is a challenge, especially when external funding conditions are uncertain. Experience from past crises like the Asian financial crisis and global financial crisis highlights the importance of strengthening domestic financial resilience to mitigate negative spillovers from changes in global funding conditions. Meanwhile, Box 5 points to the role of smoothing exchange rate fluctuations to reduce uncertainty regarding domestic financial conditions. To this end, both monetary and macroprudential policies need to consider the effects exchange rate movements have on domestic financial conditions through both the financial and trade channels. As such, domestic policies should be coordinated to ensure that they are effective, avoiding potential conflict and undesirable outcomes.

Box 5: The Influence of United States Dollar Funding Conditions on Asian Financial Markets

In a panel analysis of 20 emerging market economies, Hofmann, Shim, and Shin (2017)[a] found that local currency appreciation against the United States (US) dollar improved a country's balance sheet as the value of dollar-denominated liabilities decreased relative to assets. Appreciation also increased foreign fund flows into sovereign bonds, suppressed yield spreads between bonds denominated in local currency and foreign currency, and lowered an economy's credit risk premium, thereby loosening financial conditions. Avdjiev et al. (2018)[b] found evidence that a stronger dollar was associated with lower growth in dollar-denominated cross-border bank flows and lower real investment in emerging market economies. These findings support the view that a stronger US dollar can have real macroeconomic effects in the opposite direction to effects from the standard trade channel.

Focusing more on evidence from emerging economies in Asia, Lee, Rosenkranz, and Pham (2019)[c] estimated a dynamic panel model for eight such economies—India, Indonesia, Malaysia, the People's Republic of China, the Philippines, the Republic of Korea, Thailand, and Viet Nam—with monthly data from December 2006 to August 2018. The following equation was estimated using Anderson-Hsiao's instrumental variable estimation (Anderson and Hsiao 1982),[d] which also addressed possible endogeneity problems.

$$(1)\ \Delta y_{i,t} = \alpha_i + \delta\Delta y_{i,t-1} + \beta_1\Delta BER_{t-1} + \beta_2\Delta NEER_{i,t-1} + \gamma_1\Delta CPI_{t-1} + \gamma_2\Delta IP_{t-1} + \gamma_3\Delta r_{i,t-1} + \eta_1\Delta VIX_{t-1} + \eta_2\Delta CPIUS_{t-1} + \eta_3\Delta IPUS_{t-1} + \eta_4\Delta MMUS_{t-1} + \varepsilon_{i,t}$$

The dependent variable was defined as the change month-on-month in local currency sovereign bond spread,[e] whereby an increase indicated tightening domestic financial conditions. The main control variables were the change month-on-month in the BER against the US dollar and the change month-on-month in the NEER. Other variables included were the change month-on-month in the volatility index; change in the domestic and US consumer price index year-on-year; change in the domestic and US industrial production index year-on-year; change in the domestic lending rate month-on-month, which was defined as the average 1-year lending rate of domestic commercial banks; and change month-on-month in the 3-month money market rate in the US.

The results, in the table, point to two opposing channels of the exchange rate in play. While changes in bilateral exchange rates against the US dollar primarily affected financial conditions through the financial channel, changes in nominal effective exchange rates acted more through the trade channel.

Estimation Results: Dynamic Panel Regression

Dependent variable: change month-on-month in the local currency sovereign bond spread

$\Delta y_{i,t-1}$	0.403***	$\Delta r_{i,t-1}$	–0.00165***
$\Delta BER_{i,t-1}$	0.0424***	$\Delta VIX_{i,t-1}$	0.00114**
$\Delta NEER_{i,t-1}$	–0.0723***	$\Delta CPIUS_{i,t-1}$	0.000522
$\Delta CPI_{i,t-1}$	–0.000180	$\Delta IPUS_{i,t-1}$	–0.0231
$\Delta IP_{i,t-1}$	0.00149	$\Delta MMUS_{i,t-1}$	–0.00255

*** = significant at 1%, ** = significant at 5%, * = significant at 10%, ΔBER = log change month-on-month in the bilateral exchange rate against US dollar (an increase indicates local currency depreciation), ΔCPI, $\Delta CPIUS$ = change year-on-year in the domestic and US consumer price index, ΔIP, $\Delta IPUS$ = change year-on-year in the domestic and US industrial production index, $\Delta MMUS$ = change month-on-month in the 3-month money market rate in the US, $\Delta NEER$ = change month-on-month in the nominal effective exchange rate (an increase indicates local currency depreciation), Δr = change month-on-month in the lending rate (defined as the average 1-year lending rate of domestic commercial banks), ΔVIX = log change month-on-month in the Chicago Board Options Exchange volatility index, US = United States.

Source: Lee, J., P. Rosenkranz, and H. Pham. 2019. The Influence of US Dollar Funding Conditions on Asian Financial Markets. Background paper for Asian Development Outlook 2019 section on "Challenges from Rising Headwinds" Manuscript.

continued on next page

Box 5 *continued*

Estimation results suggested that, on average, a 1% bilateral depreciation against the US dollar tended to increase sovereign bond spreads by approximately 4.2 basis points, while a 1% currency depreciation in NEER terms tended to decrease sovereign bond spreads by approximately 7.2 basis points. Qualitatively, the regression results aligned with the findings of Hofmann, Shim, and Shin (2017).[a] The findings suggested a significant relationship between US dollar funding and domestic financial conditions in selected emerging Asian economies and highlight the vulnerabilities that stem from the region's high reliance on US dollar-denominated external funding.

[a] Hofmann, B., I. Shim, and H. S. Shin. 2017. Sovereign Yields and the Risk-Taking Channel of Currency Appreciation. *BIS Working Papers* No. 538. Bank for International Settlements.
[b] Avdjiev, S., et al. 2018. The Dollar Exchange Rate as a Global Risk Factor: Evidence from Investment. *BIS Working Papers* No. 695. Bank for International Settlements.
[c] Lee, J., P. Rosenkranz, and H. Pham. 2019. The Influence of US Dollar Funding Conditions on Asian Financial Markets. Background paper for Asian Development Outlook 2019 section on "Challenges from Rising Headwinds" Manuscript.
[d] Anderson, T. and C. Hsiao. 1982. Formulation and Estimation of Dynamic Models Using Panel Data. *Journal of Econometrics* 18 (1).
[e] The difference between the 5-year local currency sovereign bond yield and the 5-year US Treasury yield, following the definition used in Hofmann, Shim, and Shin (2017).

More broadly, further developing and deepening capital markets in the region can provide a better environment for maintaining healthy domestic financial conditions. Expanding the investor base at home and developing local currency bond markets can dampen unwanted effects from the global financial environment. To promote better domestic financial resilience and dampen the impact of external funding conditions on domestic financial markets, all these policies should go together with strengthened policy dialogue across borders to monitor macrofinancial conditions, identify systemic risks, and improve regional financing arrangements. Capital flow management measures should also be considered to mitigate disruptive spillover of capital flows in an increasingly interconnected global financial system.

Challenge of Small Open Economies in Asia: Mongolia and Cambodia

The idiosyncratic factors of small open economies require special attention.

From crisis periods, Asian small open economies have learned their lessons, including the need for country-specific policies to address imbalances (no one-size-fits-all prescriptions), the need to build up external buffers (such as reserves) during boom times, and maintaining fiscal discipline. Mongolia and Cambodia demonstrate the vulnerability of small open economies to external shocks. Appropriate policy responses aim to maintain price and financial stability and promote debt sustainability.

Mongolia's economy was vulnerable because it was heavily reliant on one sector, mining, and one trading partner, the PRC. GDP growth surged 17.3% in 2011 as commodity prices boomed. But momentum quickly dissipated and growth fell below 5% in 2015 as (i) commodity prices declined; (ii) the PRC economy slowed; and (iii) undisciplined public expenditure was carried out based on speculation about commodity prices. In addition, faulty policy measures were implemented. The new Law on Development Bank of Mongolia allowed spending to increase beyond what was stipulated in the budget. Meanwhile, the policy rate was cut substantially and, along with the new quasi-fiscal lending programs,[7] injected about 25% of GDP into the economy. The resulting credit

---

[7]   Several of these quasi-fiscal activities were carried out under the Price Stabilization Program. Others were classified as Retail Mortgage and Troubled Asset Relief Program.

boom fueled imports, leading to a sharp depreciation of the currency, the tögrög, and a depletion of foreign exchange reserves. The tögrög depreciated by an average of 10.3% from 2012 to 2017. Foreign exchange reserves fell from $3.93 billion in 2012 to $1.24 billion in 2016 before recovering to $2.84 billion in 2017.

Mongolia decided to undertake large-scale policy adjustments and structural reforms as part of the $5.5 billion IMF-led bailout package aimed to stabilize the economy, reduce debt pressure, rebuild foreign exchange reserves, and rehabilitate and reform the financial sector. In May 2017, the IMF approved the 3-year Extended Fund Facility arrangement amounting to $425 million, accompanied by strict and ambitious requirements. These included (i) strengthening budget discipline; (ii) rebuilding foreign exchange reserves; (iii) maintaining a tight monetary policy; (iv) recapitalizing and restructuring the banking system; and (v) improving governance, regulation, and supervision of banks by amending the Banking Law and the Law on Central Bank. The Bank of Mongolia has also been conducting the Asset Quality Review estimating banks' capital shortfalls and mandating banks to increase capital.

As the Extended Fund Facility was being formulated, ADB crafted a Country Partnership Strategy to help Mongolia sustain inclusive growth amid economic difficulty (ADB 2020b). To facilitate this, ADB operations were designed to focus on three strategic pillars: (i) promoting economic and social stability, (ii) developing infrastructure for economic diversification, and (iii) strengthening environmental sustainability.

Under the program with the IMF, public finances have stabilized, and growth has recovered. However, the recovery is fragile, debt-servicing costs are still high, and Mongolia remains vulnerable to fluctuations in commodity prices. The government should respond to these challenges and set the stage for more effective use of mineral resources, not by creating new funds, but by strengthening public financial management more broadly. This will become even more crucial as major mining investments advance toward their production stage, mineral revenues consequently rise, and debt service payments moderate with the implementation of the IMF stabilization program. Crucial steps toward better public financial management include bringing all spending within the budget and creating a stronger fiscal base that reduces dependence on commodity prices by, for example, amending excise and income taxes (ADB 2019a).

Meanwhile, recent financial reforms have focused on strengthening the banking system so that the bulk of lending goes not just to mining, but also to new areas of the economy, such as small and medium-sized enterprises, agriculture, and female entrepreneurs. This will help diversify the economy. The Bank of Mongolia also needs to have good, up-to-date regulations, enforce all regulations on other banks, and make sure banks have adequate capital. Bank recapitalization, initiated in 2018 by the central bank, continued into 2019.

Cambodia's economy is considered very open, with total trade at 129% of GDP in 2018 and total foreign direct inflows at 12.6% of GDP in 2018 (ADB 2019b). The downside is that external shocks are quickly transmitted to Cambodia's economy. During the global financial crisis, GDP growth fell to nearly zero, hurting three of the four pillars of Cambodia's economy: exports, construction, and tourism. The global financial crisis also exposed Cambodia's other vulnerabilities: its heavy reliance on garment exports and a heavy concentration of trade with the EU and the US. In 2017, garment exports comprised 64% of the total; and 58% of total exports went to the EU and the US.[8] After the global financial crisis, efforts have been made to reduce vulnerability in these areas, with some success in diversifying. But another area of concern has emerged: the shares of the banking sector and real estate in foreign direct investment inflows has increased. The National Bank of Cambodia has been proactive in this regard. Since 2000, it has raised minimum capital requirements of banks in 2008, 2016, and 2018 and it has been monitoring the real estate sector by establishing the property price index, the basis for the loan-to-value indicator. This allows the central bank to monitor lending risks based on the amount of mortgages.

---

[8]   Garment exports refer to textile fibers, yarn, fabrics, and clothing (totaling $7.8 million in 2017). The country's world exports amounted to $12.1 million in 2017, $2.3 million of which went to the US and $4.7 million to the EU. Data from the United Nations Conference on Trade and Development. https://unctadstat.unctad.org/EN/ (accessed 31 January 2020).

5 Policy Considerations

Policies to reduce economic vulnerabilities created by macrofinancial linkages can be categorized into domestic policies, policies requiring regional cooperation, and international policies under the label of the New Financial Regulatory Framework.

Twenty years after the Asian financial crisis, Asia stands strong—with more flexible exchange rates, healthier external and fiscal positions, stronger regulations, deeper capital markets, and better regional financial cooperation mechanisms. However, existing and newly emerging challenges[9]—largely generated by deeper financial interconnectedness—pose potential risks to financial stability in developing Asia. The COVID-19 pandemic, moreover, threatens to reverse many of the hard-won development gains across the region and exacerbate existing financial vulnerabilities. Now more than ever, policy makers must build on the reforms instituted in response to the Asian financial crisis. ADB (2017) suggests that these include (i) strengthening financial supervision and macroprudential regulations to address NPLs and restore banking sector confidence, and (ii) adopting measures to stem short-term capital outflows and raising interest rates to reduce investor flight. They also include (iii) establishing more flexible exchange rate regimes, and (iv) instituting a broader set of reforms to restructure the banking sector and develop and deepen capital markets.

The studies reviewed identify the areas which pose the more important challenges to Asia's financial stability, with several important findings. Among these, over the past 20 years, Asian financial markets have grown more interconnected, both within the region and across the globe. Growing financial interconnectedness can increase vulnerabilities to external shocks, financial contagion, or liquidity risks stemming from cross-border bank lending. In addition, continued high reliance on US dollar-denominated funding has significant implications for the transmission of global financial conditions to domestic financial and macroeconomic conditions. Finally, a sustained increase in NPLs can lead to a reduction in credit supply and slow overall economic activity. Lessons drawn from the crises and the results of empirical analyses highlight the importance of enhancing financial market resilience to safeguard Asia's financial stability. This can only work through the interplay between adequate national policies and frameworks, and efforts to continue and facilitate regional cooperation. In an increasingly interconnected global financial network, financial resilience cannot be achieved in isolation; it requires cross-border cooperation.

---

[9]   These include (i) the links between financial cycles and the real economy, (ii) more rapid risk transmission from greater financial interconnectedness, and (iii) rising volatility from macrofinancial interlinkages, among others (ADB 2017).

Domestic Policies

Microprudential and macroprudential policies are at the heart of domestic policies to maintain financial stability.

Sound macroeconomic conditions—healthy external and fiscal positions, exchange rate flexibility, a well-regulated and strong financial system, and adequate foreign exchange reserves—are central to financial resilience and economic growth. These also buffer against future crises and help soften the impact of external shocks. Targeted microprudential and macroprudential policies to curb financial excess are also needed to maintain financial stability. Given the rapidly globalizing financial landscape, important considerations for prudential supervision include strengthening bank capacity to manage foreign currency liquidity risk—for example, through monitoring and implementing a foreign currency liquidity coverage ratio. They also include consolidating supervision, ensuring adequate communication between central banks and other financial supervisors, and regulating systemically important financial institutions.

Meanwhile, authorities should consider establishing and implementing an effective macroprudential policy framework to address two dimensions of system-wide risks: (i) a buildup of a systemic risk over time (the "time dimension") and (ii) a spillover and contagion of risk across different financial sectors and systems (the "cross-sectional dimension"). Macroprudential policies can be useful in dampening the procyclicality of the financial system. Good examples are countercyclical provisions, capital and liquidity buffers, and balance sheet instruments such as leverage ratios, and limits on debt-to-income and loan-to-value ratios.

Zhang and Zoli (2014) find that over time, Asian economies appear to have made greater use of macroprudential tools, especially housing-related measures, than their counterparts in other regions. Their analysis suggests that macroprudential policy and capital flow measures have helped curb housing price growth, equity flows, credit growth, and bank leverage. Instruments such as loan-to-value ratio caps, housing tax measures, and foreign currency-related measures have been particularly effective.

Lee, Asuncion, and Kim (2016) report similar empirical results for 10 economies. For example, in 2000–2013, the People's Bank of China and the China Banking Regulatory Commission launched macroprudential instruments simultaneously to improve financial stability. They tightened macroprudential measures more than 40 times during this period; at least 31 liquidity-related instruments including reserve requirements. The results show that credit-related macroprudential tightening immediately dampened credit expansion and reduced housing price appreciation with lags, but it had no effect on leverage growth. The Reserve Bank of India has been using various macroprudential policies, including capital-related policies, since 2004 as a tool kit for ensuring financial stability. Meanwhile, to mitigate excessive investment and speculative activity in the property market and to contain substantial increases in property prices, in the fourth quarter of 2010, Bank Negara Malaysia introduced a maximum loan-to-value ratio of 70% for loans to purchase third houses.

Past crises have also underscored the need for a foreign currency funding condition to macroprudential policies. As the Asian financial crisis demonstrated, currency mismatches are a major source of risk. Given Asia's heavy reliance on US dollar-denominated debt, the region could augment existing macroprudential policy tools with, for example, a foreign currency liquidity coverage ratio. This policy tool could help the banking sector strengthen resilience against external shocks, especially during financial distress.

Domestic capital market development will also mitigate the risk of capital outflows and currency mismatch problems. A local bond market would be the natural environment to develop long-term, local currency-denominated debt instruments that would provide a more stable and reliable financing framework. Development of local currency bond markets, however, has a regional dimension which is explained in the next section.

Regional Policies

Regional policies aim mainly to help channel regional savings into regional investment projects.

More developed and regionally integrated banking sectors and financial markets can improve the efficiency of resource allocation to the real economy. Asia's vast amounts of regional savings could be better channeled into more productive investments, but this reinvestment is constrained by insufficient capital-market-based financing solutions and reliance on US dollar funding. For example, about $4.4 trillion is invested in Asia's pension funds, $5.1 trillion with insurers, and several large social security and public pension reserve funds. Yet, potential investors must often restrain investments due to concerns over political risk, weak regulatory systems, the legal environment, governance standards, and undeveloped capital markets. More developed and regionally integrated banking and financial markets can improve the efficiency of resource allocation to the real economy.

Challenges remain even though local currency bonds outstanding in ASEAN+3 increased fourfold from $6.6 trillion in 2002 to $27.4 trillion by the end of March 2020. To meet the region's financing needs, local currency bond markets must become more efficient, broaden their investor bases, deepen secondary markets, and integrate more regionally. Developing local currency bond markets will also help diversify funding sources, reduce concentrated funding risks, and provide investors long-term finance opportunities that are vital for financing long-term infrastructure projects. Many Asian economists and policy makers, however, argued that an integrated Asian bond market would be valuable in achieving such a liability structure. Following this view, Asian authorities initiated various regional initiatives to strengthen and deepen local currency bond markets. The ASEAN+3 launched the Asian Bond Markets Initiative, which focuses on the supply side or infrastructure of bond markets, including clearing and settlement systems, rating agencies, and denomination currencies. This has helped promote regional capital market development, which can help avoid maturity and currency mismatches.

Strengthening policy dialogue and cooperation globally and regionally, meanwhile, is essential for enhancing Asia's financial resilience. Its financial markets are increasingly open, interconnected, and vulnerable to external shocks, and approaching challenges from a regional perspective helps build financial resilience. A regional cooperation mechanism on macroprudential policy frameworks, for example, could safeguard financial stability.

An important lesson from the European debt crisis is that regional cooperation to develop effective resolution mechanisms for distressed assets of cross-border financial institutions is important to broader financial safety net arrangements. With greater financial integration, banks increasingly operate internationally. Growing regional banking activities and institutions—possibly of systemic importance—underpin the need to discuss regional regulatory cooperation, including resolution mechanisms for interconnected regional banks—such as Qualified ASEAN Banks. In this increasingly interconnected environment, the failure of a single regional bank could have considerable negative impact on economies in emerging Asia. Measures that identify and effectively deal with vulnerabilities in systemically important financial institutions would thus be key to reducing systemic risk and their associated moral hazards. Regional cooperation to develop effective resolution mechanisms for distressed assets of cross-border financial institutions can also complement national efforts to address NPLs efficiently and sustainably. In addition, developing both distressed asset markets and financial market infrastructure nationally can deepen financial markets and enhance market resilience, helping strengthen the multilayered regional financial safety net.

As highlighted in section IV, the systemic importance of foreign banks in Asia is growing. Stable funding through foreign bank credit supply channels to a host economy remains a key issue for financial stability. Supervisory colleges for regionally active foreign banks can be an effective regional cooperation tool to strengthen cross-border supervision in Asia.[10] They can enhance understanding and oversight of the sources and transmission channels of systemic risks and shocks.

The New Financial Regulatory Framework

The global financial crisis revealed regulatory gaps, ineffective monitoring, opaque markets, and financial products that were too complex to manage.

In the aftermath of the global financial crisis, many financial reforms were introduced, including major new institutions or new frameworks. Among the more important ones are:

Financial Stability Board. Established in April 2009 as a successor to the Financial Stability Forum, the organization promotes international financial stability. It does so by coordinating national financial authorities and international standard-setting bodies as they work toward developing strong regulatory, supervisory, and other financial sector policies. It fosters a level playing field by encouraging coherent implementation of these policies across sectors and jurisdictions.

Basel Committee on Banking Supervision. This is a committee of banking supervisory authorities established by the central bank governors of the Group of Ten countries in 1974. The committee expanded its membership in 2009 after the global financial crisis and then again in 2014.

Basel III: A global regulatory framework for more resilient banks and banking systems. This was the most important contribution of the committee in response to the global financial crisis. Basel III addresses shortcomings in the pre-crisis regulatory framework and provides a foundation for a resilient banking system that will help avoid the buildup of systemic vulnerabilities. The framework will allow the banking system to support the real economy through the economic cycle.

Managing Capital Flows

Tools for managing capital flows considered mainstream have increased in number as capital management techniques have gained acceptance.

Global capital flows, which benefit and challenge Asian economies, are another indicator of deeper global financial integration. Figure 8 shows that non-resident flows to emerging Asia rose prior to the global financial crisis and in response to the quantitative easing in the US. This reflects the volatility of capital flows. Policy responses to deal with volatility and maintain financial stability dovetail with the recommendations detailed earlier in this section.

Policy makers need only to be reminded that a "sudden stop" of capital flows was a key factor in the Asian financial crisis. The impact of capital flows on the exchange rate is at the heart of the discussion of appropriate policy responses in emerging markets. If capital flows are driven largely by fundamentals—such as a higher Wicksellian "natural" interest rate or the Balassa-Samuelson effect—authorities must accept the inevitability of allowing the real exchange rate to appreciate. In fact, real exchange appreciation is the only sustainable response

---

[10]   In general, supervisory colleges are permanent but flexible structures for collaboration, coordination, and information-sharing among the authorities responsible for and involved in the supervision of cross-border banking groups. Bank for International Settlements. 2014. *Basel Committee on Banking Supervision: Principles for Effective Supervisory Colleges.* Basel.

Figure 8: Non-Resident Flows—Emerging Asia
($ million)

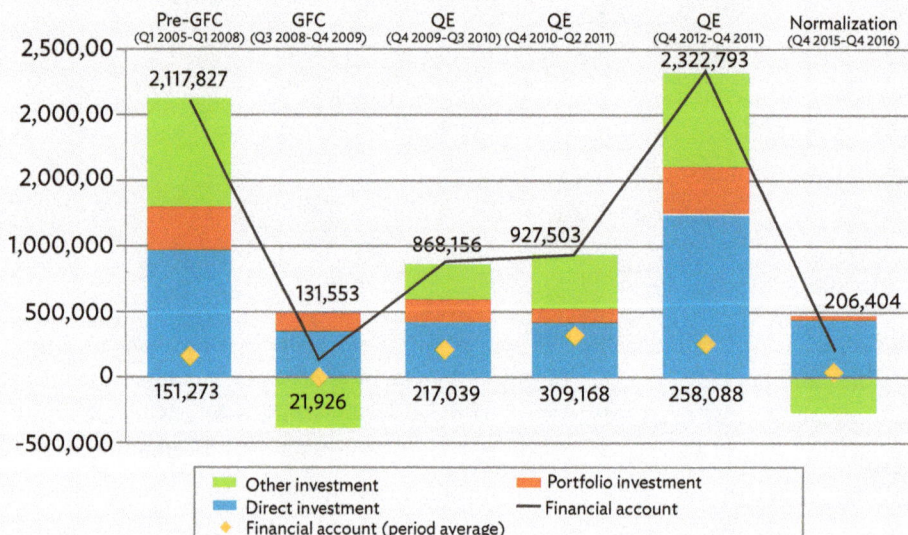

GFC = global financial crisis, QE = quantitative easing.

Notes:

1. Break in comparability of data for the Philippines (2005), India (2009), Brunei Darussalam (2010), and Malaysia (2010). For Malaysia, this effectively discounts "other investment" in its assets and liabilities breakdown.
2. For the consistency of the chart, net of "other investment" corresponds to resident inflows for Malaysia starting 2010.
3. In the case of the Lao People's Democratic Republic, net of direct, portfolio, and other investment corresponds to non-resident inflows direct, portfolio, and other investment starting 2014.
4. Emerging Asia excludes Cambodia starting first quarter (Q1) of 2015; and Brunei Darussalam, Myanmar, and Viet Nam for Q1 2016.

Source: Villafuerte, J. 2017. Managing Capital Flows to Emerging Asia. Background paper for Asian Economic Integration Report 2017 Theme Chapter on "The Era of Financial Interconnectedness: How Can Asia Strengthen Financial Resilience?" Manuscript.

to a permanent increase in capital inflows and a fundamental revaluation of domestic relative to foreign assets (Kawai and Takagi 2010). However, policy makers are generally reluctant to allow currencies to appreciate.

Three broad categories of macroeconomic measures are available to countries facing surges of capital inflows, if they are not willing to allow the nominal exchange rate to appreciate. These are (i) sterilized intervention, (ii) greater exchange rate flexibility, and (iii) fiscal tightening (preferably through an expenditure cut). Table 2 summarizes the relevant issues for each with more details in Kawai and Takagi (2010).

Because the policy responses presented in Table 2 have their respective drawbacks, the issue of capital management techniques—a euphemism for capital controls—has remained relevant. Moreover, the experience with the Asian financial crisis and other similar crises has shifted the policy debate. Whereas, free flows previously dominated the analytical and intellectual debate, the current thinking has moved toward policy intervention. It has been observed that past aversion to capital management techniques has seemingly been replaced with a new appreciation of its contribution to economic policy as a tool for financial stability.

However, the current positions "seem to be transitional rather than conceptually well founded" (Grenville 2012). The best example of this is the position of the IMF, which essentially acknowledges that temporary management of capital flows may be necessary, but only after all other possible measures have been exhausted. However, this new framework has been described as complicated, intentionally vague, and difficult to implement given the absence of explicit guidelines (Gochoco-Bautista and Rhee 2013).

Table 2: Summary of Policy Measures

	Policy Tools	Intended Outcome	Possible Limitations	Evidence on Effectiveness	Recommended Policy Responses
Macroeconomic Measures	Sterilized intervention	Prevent nominal and real appreciation while neutralizing the growth of base money	Rising quasi–fiscal cost; higher interest rates that attract additional inflows; unable to prevent real appreciation over the medium term due to eventual inflation	Some evidence of effectiveness in the short term, but not in the medium to long term	Limit the use of sterilized intervention as a short-run measure; reduce international reserves through a reserve–sharing arrangement (like a multilateralized Chiang Mai Initiative)
	Greater exchange rate flexibility	Direct monetary policy for macroeconomic management; discourage speculative capital inflows by creating two-way risks	Loss of international price competitiveness	Limited evidence on the response of speculative flows	Allow greater flexibility through regional cooperation (see the discussion on regional collective action)
	Fiscal policy tightening	Contain inflationary pressure; discourage capital inflows by reducing interest rate pressure; prevent real appreciation	Lack of flexibility and timeliness; a natural limit to the degree of tightening; reduction of the provision of some basic services and infrastructure investment; possibility of a positive signaling effect to attract additional inflows	Some evidence of effectiveness in preventing real appreciation and keeping better growth performance following capital flow reversals	Exploit the automatic stabilizer function of the budget; that is, the government may implement planned infrastructure investment and basic services delivery without increasing spending out of higher tax revenues or reducing tax rates

continued on next page

Table 2 continued

continued on next page

Policy Tools	Intended Outcome	Possible Limitations	Evidence on Effectiveness	Recommended Policy Responses
Financial sector reform	Minimize the negative impact of capital flow reversals by promoting risk management	Not achievable in the short run	Not applicable	Strengthen financial sector supervision and regulation; develop and deepen capital markets
Controls on capital inflows	Limit capital inflows	High administrative capacity required, which is lacking in many emerging market economies	Some evidence of effectiveness in lengthening the maturity of inflows without much impact on the volume; effectiveness tends to weaken over time	For financially open economies, carefully design selective, temporary, market-based controls and avoid a system of extensive administrative controls. For financially closed economies, pursue capital account liberalization in a well-sequenced way together with institutional development
Easing restrictions on capital outflows	Reduce net inflows by encouraging outflows; allow residents to diversify risks	Insufficient pent-up demand for foreign assets; possibility of a positive signaling effect to attract additional inflows	Some evidence of promoting additional capital inflows	Ease outflow controls together with complementary measures such as strengthening financial sector supervision
Rebalancing growth	Reduce current account surpluses by refocusing sources of growth from external to domestic demand; contain upward pressure on the real exchange rate	Policy makers' reluctance to abandon existing policies	Not applicable	For former crisis economies, stimulate infrastructure investment. For the People's Republic of China, reduce corporate and household savings and redirect investment toward social sector protection
Further trade liberalization	Reduce current account surpluses by encouraging imports; contain upward pressure on the real exchange rate	Failure of net imports to rise when the tradables sector becomes more competitive as a result; possibility of a positive signaling effect to attract additional inflows	Not applicable	Sustain ongoing efforts to liberalize trade

Structural Measures

Table 2 *continued*

Collective Action	Policy Tools	Intended Outcome	Possible Limitations	Evidence on Effectiveness	Recommended Policy Responses
Global solutions	Greater transparency	Minimize the volatility of capital flows by strengthening the role of fundamentals	Lack of sufficient attention to fundamentals by market participants	Occurrence of crises despite the rise in transparency	Support ongoing international transparency initiatives
Global solutions	Counter-cyclicality in financial regulation	Minimize herd behavior resulting from imperfect and asymmetric information	Unlikely to receive wide support	Not applicable	Consider this measure as part of the agenda for future research
Regional solutions	Regional exchange rate coordination	Maintain macroeconomic and financial sector stability without much affecting international price competitiveness	Not viable without a mechanism for conducting intensive policy dialogue and cooperation	Not applicable	Utilize existing policy dialogue processes such as ASEAN+3 Economic Review and Policy Dialogue (ERPD) and Executives' Meeting of East Asia and Pacific Central Banks (EMEAP) to achieve collective currency appreciation
Regional solutions	Regional financial market surveillance and/or integration	Monitor regional financial markets and capital flows; mitigate the impact of investor herd behavior and financial contagion	Not viable without an effective institution	Not applicable	Establish a new, high-level "Asian Financial Stability Dialogue" on regional financial sector issues
Regional solutions	Regional cooperation on capacity building	Enhance capacity of financial regulators and supervisors to manage increasing financial risks in the markets	Not viable without an effective institution	Not applicable	Include this measure among important functions of the Asian Financial Stability Dialogue

ASEAN+3 = Association of Southeast Asian Nations plus Japan, the People's Republic of China, and the Republic of Korea.

Source: Kawai, M. and M. B. Lamberte. 2010. Managing Capital Flows: Emerging Asia's Experiences, Policy Issues and Challenges. In M. Kawai and M. B. Lamberte, eds. *Managing Capital Flows: The Search for a Framework*. Edward Elgar Publishing Limited. Table 1.9, pp. 35–38.

Meanwhile, macroprudential policy can safeguard financial stability, in particular, to deal with the credit and asset price cycles driven by global capital flows (Zhang and Zoli 2014). The Asian financial crisis and global financial crisis showed that macroprudential policy can be implemented to prevent financial volatility from overcoming sound macroeconomic fundamentals.

Financial Technology

In general, technological developments have not yet resulted in any major upheaval in the structure of financial regulation, but it would be prudent for policy makers to be forward looking.

Faced with the risks brought about by financial innovation, regulators have responded with similar regulatory innovations. Challenges posed by regulatory arbitrage and limited knowledge of fintech activities can be solved with innovation offices and regulatory sandboxes. Innovation offices provide an avenue for regulator–innovator engagement. Engaging with the fintech industry helps regulators understand key trends and the potential issues and risks of innovative financial services and their implications for regulatory policy.

Resource constraints for emerging and developing economies, though not directly addressed, can be mitigated through regional knowledge-sharing and policy dialogue, such as the ASEAN+3 Economic Review and Policy Dialogue. Efficient and effective policies and regulations can be implemented directly using the experience of more developed economies or through other knowledge-sharing policy platforms. Tangentially, the coordination provided by regional knowledge sharing and policy dialogue may reduce the potential for regulatory arbitrage by creating uniform international best practices in formulating policies and regulations.

Meanwhile, FSB (2019a) identifies three issues that may be worthy of further consideration by policy makers:

(i)   The presence of Big Tech firms in financial services may also highlight the need to complement an entity-based approach with an activity-based approach to regulation, to ensure appropriate and consistent coverage of activities that have implications for financial stability.

(ii) The diverse business lines of Big Tech firms, coupled with their complex and varied interlinkages with traditional financial institutions, may be a source of risk. Financial sector regulators and supervisors should be mindful of—and should continue to monitor—these linkages, including the effect of Big Tech firms' activities on incumbent financial institutions' ability to generate capital via retained profits.

(iii) Big Tech firms' ability to leverage customer data may raise the question of how financial authorities should approach data rights, particularly in the wider context of data protection regulations. Regulatory obligations for banks to share relevant data with new entrants (such as that embodied in open banking regulations) may enhance competition, but may also pose new risks.

References

Anderson, T. and C. Hsiao. 1982. Formulation and Estimation of Dynamic Models Using Panel Data. *Journal of Econometrics* 18 (1).

Asian Development Bank (ADB). 2017. *Asian Economic Integration Report 2017: The Era of Financial Interconnectedness, How Can Asia Strengthen Financial Resilience?* Manila.

———. 2019a. *Asian Development Outlook 2019: Strengthening Disaster Resilience* (April). Manila.

———. 2019b. *Asian Economic Integration Report 2019/2020: Demographic Change, Productivity, and the Role of Technology*. Manila.

———. 2020a. COVID-19 Exposes Asian Banks' Vulnerability to US Dollar Funding. *ADB Briefs*. Manila.

———. 2020b. Mongolia, 2017–2020—Sustaining Inclusive Growth in a Period of Economic Difficulty. *ADB Country Partnership Strategy*. Manila.

Avdjiev, S. et al. 2018. The Dollar Exchange Rate as a Global Risk Factor: Evidence from Investment. *BIS Working Papers* No. 695. Bank for International Settlements.

Bank for International Settlements. 2014. *Basel Committee on Banking Supervision: Principles for Effective Supervisory Colleges*. Basel.

Bernanke, B. S. and A. Blinder. 1988. Credit, Money, and Aggregate Demand. *American Economic Review*. 78 (2). pp. 435–439.

Borio, C. and H. Zhu. 2012. Capital Regulation, Risk-Taking and Monetary Policy: A Missing Link in the Transmission Mechanism? *Journal of Financial Stability*. 8 (4). pp. 236–251.

Buckley, R. P., E. Avgouleas, and D. W. Arner. 2020. Three Decades of International Financial Crises: What Have We Learned and What Still Needs to Be Done? *ADB Economics Working Paper* No. 615. Manila.

Calvi, R. 2010. Assessing Financial Integration: A Comparison between Europe and East Asia. *European Union Economic Papers*. No. 423.

Claessens, S. 2017. Financial Cycles and Crises in Asia. Background paper for Asian Economic Integration Report 2017 Theme Chapter on "The Era of Financial Interconnectedness: How Can Asia Strengthen Financial Resilience?" Manuscript.

Claessens, S. and L. Kodres. 2017. The Regulatory Responses to the Global Financial Crisis: Some Uncomfortable Questions. In E. J. Balleisen, et al., eds. *Policy Shock: Recalibrating Risk and Regulation after Oil Spills, Nuclear Accidents and Financial Meltdowns Crises.* pp. 435–484. New York: Cambridge University Press.

Claessens, S. et al. 2014. Introduction in S. Claessens, et al., eds. *Financial Crises: Causes, Consequences, and Policy Responses.* pp. xiii–xxvi. Washington, DC: International Monetary Fund.

Claessens, S., M. A. Kose, and M. E. Terrones. 2012. How do Business and Financial Cycles Interact? *Journal of International Economics.* 87 (1). pp. 178–190.

Claessens, S. and M. A. Kose. 2018. Frontiers of Macrofinancial Linkages. *Bank for International Settlements Papers.* No. 95 (January). Basel: Bank for International Settlements.

Dungey, M. et al. 2017. The Changing Network of Financial Market Linkages: The Asian Experience. Background paper for Asian Economic Integration Report 2017 Theme Chapter on "The Era of Financial Interconnectedness: How Can Asia Strengthen Financial Resilience?" Manuscript.

Financial Stability Board (FSB). 2019a. *BigTech in Finance: Market Developments and Potential Financial Stability Implications.* 9 December. Basel: Financial Stability Board.

———. 2019b. *FinTech and Market Structure in Financial Services: Market Developments and Potential Financial Stability Implications.* 14 February. Basel: Financial Stability Board.

Gochoco-Bautista, M. S. and C. Rhee. 2013. Capital Controls: A Pragmatic Proposal. *ADB Economics Working Paper Series.* No. 337. Manila: Asian Development Bank.

Greenwald, B. C. and J. E. Stiglitz. 1993. Financial Market Imperfections and Business Cycles. *Quarterly Journal of Economics.* 108 (1). pp. 77–114.

Grenville, S. 2012. Rethinking Capital Flows for Emerging Asia. *ADBI Working Paper Series.* No. 262 (June).

Hofmann, B., I. Shim, and H. S. Shin. 2017. Sovereign Yields and the Risk-Taking Channel of Currency Appreciation. *BIS Working Papers* No. 538. Bank for International Settlements.

Kawai, M. and M. B. Lamberte. 2010. Managing Capital Flows: Emerging Asia's Experiences, Policy Issues and Challenges. In M. Kawai and M. B. Lamberte, eds. *Managing Capital Flows: The Search for a Framework.* Edward Elgar Publishing Limited.

Kawai, M. and S. Takagi. 2010. A Survey of the Literature on Managing Capital Inflows. In M. Kawai and M. B. Lamberte, eds. *Managing Capital Flows: The Search for a Framework.* Edward Elgar Publishing Limited.

Kiyotaki, N. and J. Moore. 1997. Credit Cycles. *Journal of Political Economy.* 105 (2). pp. 211–248.

Lee, J. and P. Rosenkranz. 2019. Nonperforming Loans in Asia: Determinants and Macrofinancial Linkages. *ADB Economics Working Paper Series.* No. 574. Manila: Asian Development Bank.

Lee, J., P. Rosenkranz, and H. Pham. 2019. The Influence of US Dollar Funding Conditions on Asian Financial Markets. Background paper for Asian Development Outlook 2019 section on "Challenges from Rising Headwinds" Manuscript.

Lee, M., R. C. Asuncion, and J. Kim. 2016. Effectiveness of Macroprudential Policy in Developing Asia: An Empirical Analysis. *Emerging Markets Finance and Trade.* 52 (4). pp. 923–937.

Martin, R. 2017. *The Resolution of Nonperforming Loans.* Presentation at the International Public Asset Management Company Forum Research Dissemination Workshop. Manila. 30 May.

McCawley, P. 2017. The Asian Financial Crisis. In P. McCawley. *Banking on the Future of Asia and the Pacific: 50 Years of the Asian Development Bank.* Mandaluyong City: Asian Development Bank.

Mian, A., A. Sufi, and E. Verner. 2017. Household Debt and Business Cycles Worldwide. *Quarterly Journal of Economics.* 132 (4). pp. 1,755–1,817.

Obstfeld, M. and K. Rogoff. 2002. Global Implications of Self-Oriented National Monetary Rules. *Quarterly Journal of Economics.* 117 (2). pp. 503–535.

Park, C. Y. et al. 2017. 20 Years after the Asian Financial Crisis: Lessons Learned and Future Challenges. *ADB Briefs.* No. 85. Manila: Asian Development Bank.

Park, C. Y. and K. Shin. 2017. A Contagion through Exposure to Foreign Banks during the Global Financial Crisis. *ADB Economics Working Paper Series.* No. 516. Manila: Asian Development Bank.

———. 2018. Global Banking Network and Regional Financial Contagion. *ADB Economics Working Paper Series.* No. 546. Manila: Asian Development Bank.

Shim, I. and K. Shin. 2018. Financial Stress in Lender Countries and Capital Outflows from Emerging Market Economies. *Bank for International Settlements Working Papers.* No. 745. Basel: Bank for International Settlements.

Tille, C. 2008. Financial Integration and the Wealth Effect of Exchange Rate Fluctuations. *Journal of International Economics.* 75 (2). pp. 283–294.

Tille, C. and E. Van Wincoop. 2014. Solving DSGE Portfolio Choice Models with Dispersed Private Information. *Journal of Economic Dynamics and Control.* 40 (C). pp. 1–24.

Villafuerte, J. 2017. Managing Capital Flows to Emerging Asia. Background paper for Asian Economic Integration Report 2017 Theme Chapter on "The Era of Financial Interconnectedness: How Can Asia Strengthen Financial Resilience?" Manuscript.

Zhang, L. and E. Zoli. 2014. Leaning against the Wind: Macroprudential Policy in Asia. *International Monetary Fund Working Paper.* No. WP/14/22 (February). Washington, DC: International Monetary Fund.